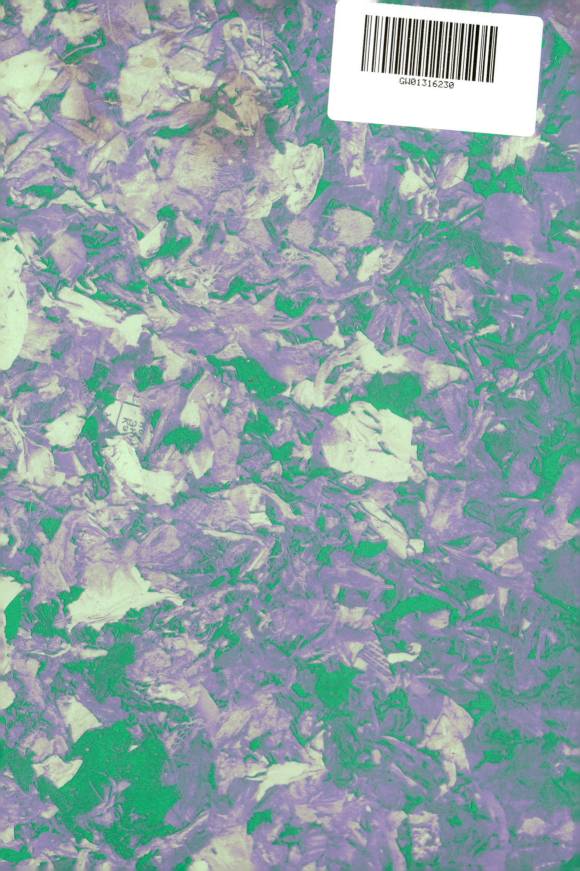

Ellen MacArthur Foundation Publishing
The Sail Loft
42 Medina Road
Cowes PO31 7BX
United Kingdom

www.ellenmacarthurfoundation.org

A catalogue record for this book is available
from the British Library.

Copyright @ Ellen MacArthur Foundation 2021

ISBN - 978-1-912737-08-6

All rights reserved. No part of this publication may be copied, extracted, reproduced, stored in a retrieval system or transmitted in any form by any means (electronic, mechanical or otherwise) without the prior written consent of the Ellen MacArthur Foundation.

Printed in Oxford, United Kingdom

The printing process used to make this book has been carefully elaborated by Seacourt, a UK-based printer that has spent the last 25 years developing a Planet Positive Printing process.
    This printing process is 100% waterless, 100% IPA (isopropyl alcohol) and IPA substitute free and is run on 100% renewable energy. The papers used are 100% recycled and zero waste was directed to landfill.
    The paper has been laminated using Cellogreen to make sure the book lasts longer without using harmful chemicals.
    Seacourt's production is net carbon positive. The company not only takes responsibility for its factory and staff's journeys but its whole supplier base as well and offsets its carbon responsibility, plus 10%.

ELLEN MACARTHUR FOUNDATION

CIRCULAR DESIGN FOR FASHION

In support of this book

"Now, more than ever, there is a need to help the fashion industry accelerate towards a more circular system, and our main goal should remain to develop and support more responsible, conscious, and resilient businesses. With the involvement and commitment of some of the most creative and innovative minds, the acceleration to a circular fashion economy is an exciting and invigorating challenge, and an essential transformation to future-proof the industry."

Caroline Rush CBE
Chief Executive Officer
British Fashion Council

"Circularity must evolve beyond a buzzword until it consciously becomes our collective way of life. Stakeholders must be deliberate about co-creating lasting solutions to help us transition to a responsible future for all – a circular economy with respect for people, resources, and the environment."

Omoyemi Akerele
Founder and Executive Director
Style House Files
Lagos Fashion Week

"An essential and stimulating challenge for today and tomorrow is to engage with creativity in fashion and with innovation to achieve sustainable development. Creativity stands for renewal and experiment, and embracing circularity models has naturally become a hugely resourceful way to transform the fashion industry."

Pascal Morand
Executive President
Fédération de la Haute Couture et de la Mode

"There is an old saying from ancient China: *strengthen the foundation and avoid waste while using* (强本而节用). It is the idea of achieving a sustainable balance between economic development and consumption. Design plays a vital role in making the best use of the material. The awareness of circularity should be placed at the forefront of design. From product design to the production process, distribution, and use, fashion brands need to join hands to make real contributions to breaking the traditional linear economic model. The establishment of effective standards can help us keep to this path and go further."

Xiaolei LYU
Deputy Secretary-General
Shanghai Fashion Week Organization

"Circular fashion must be a priority for our industry. It is one of the most important business transformations needed in how products are designed and developed. The path to a sustainable fashion industry requires a real rethinking of how clothes are valued and the creation of a marketplace where reuse is the standard."

Steven Kolb
Chief Executive Officer
Council of Fashion
Designers of America

"The circular economy is one of the most relevant frameworks to tackle our current global challenges. The fashion industry, thanks to its creativity, can become the driving force for this big change, for better and fairer ways of living, and a thriving environment. A new era begins!"

Carlo Capasa
Chairman
Camera Nazionale della Moda Italiana

"Education around circularity through design in fashion is key to supporting transformation in our industry."

Xavier Romatet
Dean of Institut Français
de la Mode

"Design is at the heart of our industry and can become the driving force behind the implementation of circularity. How do we manage the transformation without curbing creativity? Rather, how can we stimulate opportunities, innovations, and masterpieces? This beautiful and inspirational book accompanies not only designers but also all industry stakeholders, step-by-step, as they learn this new circular mindset for tomorrow's fashion."

Andrée-Anne Lemieux
Head of Sustainability IFM-KERING:
Research Chair
Institut Français de la Mode

"Fashion is not only about cultural identity, it is about the evolution of human civilisation. By innovating and transitioning the fashion industry towards a circular economy, we will create a pathway for human beings to face global challenges and share a positive common future."

Dr. Jun Li
Dean
Shanghai International College
of Fashion and Innovation
Donghua University

"As a postgraduate-level educator, circularity and sustainability-related issues rise to the top of our program applicants' concerns and remain there for the duration of our curriculum. As our students are industry professionals who attend class in the evening, they are pragmatic in their approach to implementing innovative and creative management ideas as they approach executive-level positions in industry. This important book provided by the Ellen MacArthur Foundation will be a valuable and authoritative resource in charting a course for their companies and customers, and, in that way, will influence others to learn and participate."

Pamela Ellsworth
Associate Professor and Chair
Global Fashion Management
School of Graduate Studies
Fashion Institute of Technology
State University of New York

"Circularity in fashion is of utmost importance in today's day and age. We can no longer ignore the impact of linear models on the people and the planet. It is inevitable for brands and designers to evaluate their design and production processes through the lens of the circular economy principles."

Jaspreet Chandok
Head of Lifestyle Businesses
RISE Worldwide
Lakmé Fashion Week

A change is happening, let's create it.

Ferdinando Verderi

We are an industry of desire. We create desire, we value desire, we live by desire. We understand desire is everything, and we know how to use it: communities gather around our dreams. We now have the responsibility to put our talent to service the greater good, directing desire towards something we all need, a better world. It is the best way, and soon the only way, to make our industry more relevant, more useful, and more sustainable.

Design less

The world wants less, so do we.
> We desire what we can't have. Scarcity is at the core of our business model, and today, it happens to be a meaningful tool for change. Let's celebrate rarity and uniqueness as a creative force, a commitment, a sign of integrity.

Design better

The world wants quality, so do we.
> Quality equals timelessness. Timelessness equals a lifelong emotional connection. When something lasts forever, it lives more lives, it collects stories, it connects to many. Let's create narratives around clothes that outlive us.

Design knowing

The world wants knowledge, so do we.
> We need to know before we act. We need to understand before we judge. Let's promote a culture of transparency in which information becomes a creative tool and processes become stories.

Design values

The world wants values, so do we.
> And it's no coincidence. We are witnessing an epochal shift in what we value, which we have the opportunity to embrace. Let's write a new system of identity, which recognises social beliefs as a form of beauty.

Design together

The world wants us together, so do we.
> The next generation values collaboration more than any other form of creation. Ownership is obsolete, sharing is the way forward. Our ideas together are stronger than alone: the courage to partner on meaningful ideals generates newness.

Foreword   Sara Sozzani Maino

Fashion is an industry of dreams, desire, beauty, and love for our craft.

It is an industry that prides itself on creativity, courage, and invention, and those qualities are needed now more than ever, as we rise to meet the challenges ahead.

As the Head of Vogue Talents, which celebrated its tenth anniversary in 2019, I have been privileged to witness and celebrate the positive power of design and the evolution of creative priorities for new designers. Creating an industry that is restorative and regenerative continues to rise to the top of this list.

Now is the time to reinvent ourselves even further. The circular economy can take us beyond simply trying to do less harm — it is a bigger idea, one that has the power to inspire a new generation of designers. As this book sets out, it is an opportunity to create a fashion industry that is part of the solution to challenges like climate change, biodiversity loss, waste, and pollution, and an industry that can thrive in the long term.

No generation before us has this creative opportunity and responsibility. And we are the ones who will make it happen. Together.

Part 1.
Introduction

Part 2.
Three myths and three truths about circular design

Part 3.
Designing using systems thinking

017

The fashion industry needs a redesign

035

Circular design combines circular economy principles and systems thinking

---
043

Three myths: it is all about recycling, durability, or products

---
054

Three truths: it is about collaboration, iteration, and going on a journey

---
084

What is systems thinking?

087

Redesigning supply chains, not just products

093

Designing with people and for people

Part 4.
Designing with three principles in mind

Part 5.
How to get started

Part 6.
Conclusion

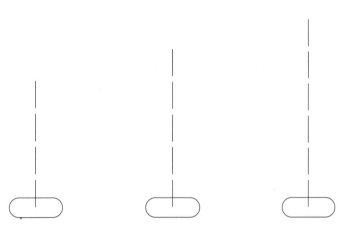

115

Eliminate waste
and pollution

185

A four-phase circular
design process

196

Advice from
our contributors

133

Circulate products
and materials

192

Questions to keep
in mind on the three
principles

207

Closing words
by Susannah Frankel

165

Regenerate nature

Who is this book for?

At heart, this book aims to inspire fearless innovators committed to spearheading the future of fashion. It is for all of us looking to make a positive impact in an industry that we love and care about.

It is increasingly acknowledged that the practice of design is not exclusive to designers, nor is it found only in studios. The materials, garments, services, shows, supply chains and stores that make up the fashion industry all work the way they do because of innumerable design decisions, made by creatives all over the world. Circular design goes far beyond rethinking single products or services, it has the potential to redefine how the entire fashion system operates. It's a chance for anyone in the fashion industry — regardless of job title — to support the shift to a circular economy where, by design, waste and pollution are eliminated, products and materials are circulated, and nature is regenerated.

Circular design is a pioneering practice of design. It is the creative opportunity of the coming decade for the creatives, innovators, and pioneers who seek to reshape the fashion industry.

About
this book

This book invites you to embark on a journey towards the future of design. It has been written in recognition of fashion's huge potential to shift towards a circular economy and in homage to its creatives — passionate disruptors on the constant search for reinvention.

It presents a new mindset.
> This book offers a creative lens through which to discover and develop new products and navigate radical transformation, while addressing many of the world's most pressing challenges.

It contributes to a growing global circular design movement.
> Design decisions shape how we interact with the world around us, and creatives across every industry and demographic are embracing their role in reimagining products, services, and systems.

It provides insights from more than 80 early practitioners of circular design in the fashion industry.
> They include established luxury brands such as Gucci and Vivienne Westwood, independent labels like Kevin Germanier and MARINE SERRE, high-street giants including Gap and H&M, pioneers of the virtual fashion experience like Alvanon and The Fabricant, and clothing resale specialists such as thredUP and Vestiaire Collective. While achieving a completely circular economy will take time, these practitioners have all started their journey. Their perspectives and insights have helped build a rich understanding of circular design and what it means for the fashion industry.

It is a gateway to a world of creativity.
> It seeks to ignite curiosity, giving the inspiration and encouragement to explore, learn, and cultivate a new design mindset.

This book has been co-created with

adidas
ADIFF
Aditya Birla Fashion and Retail Ltd (ABFRL)
Alvanon
Art Partner
ASOS
Atelier & Repairs
Bank & Vogue
Bethany Williams
Browns
Burberry
Bureau Betak
By Rotation
Candiani Denim
Circular Systems
Critical Textile Topologies
DressX
Duran Lantink
Eileen Fisher
Eon
FarFarm
Fast Retailing
Ferdinando Verderi
FFORA
Fibershed
Gabriela Hearst
Gap
Germanier
Good American
Gucci
H&M Group
Hallotex
Hirdaramani
ICICLE
I:Collect
IDEO
Inditex-Oysho
Jaypore
Kering
klee klee
La Bouche Rouge
Lacoste
Maggie Marilyn
MARINE SERRE
Month Day Year
Nkwo Onwuka
Orange Culture
Patrick McDowell
Pepijn van Eeden
Phipps International
Point Off View by Marina Testino
Powered by People
Proclaim
Provenance
PVH Corp. / Tommy Hilfiger
QAALDESIGNS
Reclothing Bank
Redress
Renewcell
RSA
RÆBURN
SAMUEL GUÌ YANG
Sara Maino
Sellalong
Shantanu & Nikhil
Sid Lee
Stella McCartney
Style House Files — Lagos Fashion Week
Susannah Frankel
Taylor Stitch
Teemill
The African Rack
The Fabricant
The Renewal Workshop
The Restory
The Sustainable Angle | Future Fabrics Expo
ThredUP
Tillmann Lauterbach
Timberland
Unmade
Vestiaire Collective
VF Corp / Napapijri
Vivienne Westwood
WGSN
W.L. Gore & Associates
YCloset
Yehyehyeh
YKK

**About the
Ellen MacArthur
Foundation**

The Ellen MacArthur Foundation is an international charity committed to the creation of a circular economy that tackles some of the biggest challenges of our time, such as climate change and biodiversity loss. Driven by design, a circular economy eliminates waste and pollution, circulates products and materials, and regenerates nature, creating benefits for society, the environment and the economy.
       This book is part of the Ellen MacArthur Foundation's Circular Design Programme, which aims to empower and equip the world's designers and creatives in fashion, food, packaging, and beyond, to embrace the circular economy opportunity.

Further information:
www.ellenmacarthurfoundation.org
@circulareconomy

INTRODUCTION

"Circular design offers us a truly meaningful challenge, one with the creative licence to rethink everything we do and why we do it. Right now is the most exciting time to be a fashion creative."

Lorna Hall
Director Fashion Intelligence
WGSN

THE FASHION INDUSTRY NEEDS A REDESIGN

Fashion is a striking example of a take-make-waste industry in which resources are used to make products that are worn very little and ultimately thrown away. It's a linear model — a one-way street.

WE HAVE NEVER PRODUCED MORE CLOTHES.

WE HAVE NEVER WORN THEM LESS.

● The industry is producing twice as many clothes as it was in the early 2000s[1] but the number of times each garment is worn has decreased significantly.[2]

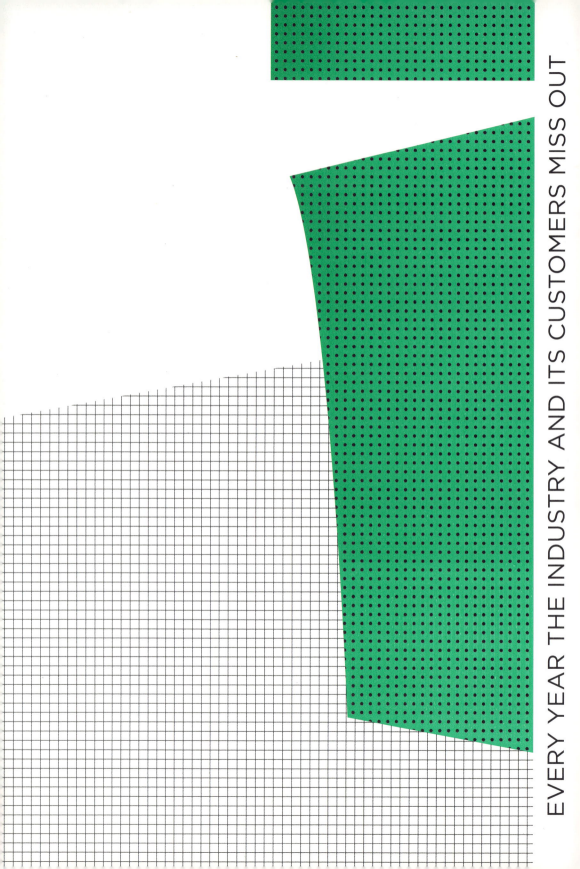
EVERY YEAR THE INDUSTRY AND ITS CUSTOMERS MISS OUT

ON HUNDREDS OF BILLIONS OF DOLLARS.

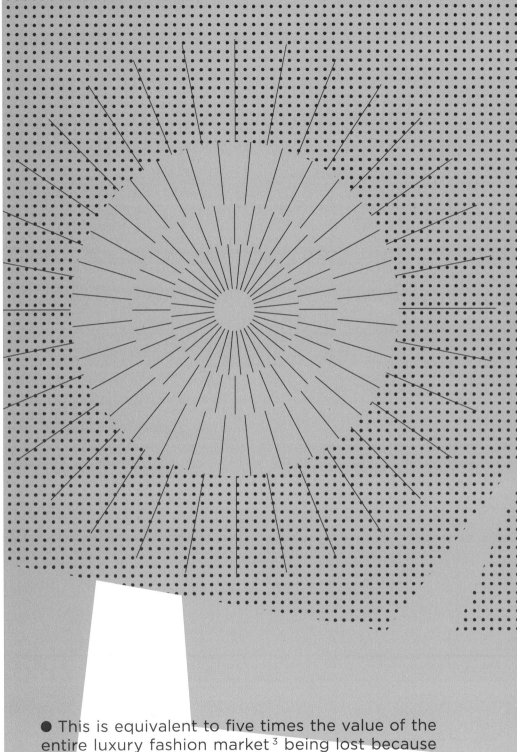

● This is equivalent to five times the value of the entire luxury fashion market[3] being lost because clothes are not worn or are discarded early.[4] It is estimated that some garments are discarded after just seven to ten wears.[5]

MOST CLOTHES AND ACCESSORIES BECOME WASTE.

● Of all the materials used to make clothes, 87% end up in landfill or are burned,[6] and only a small percentage of those that are recycled are turned into new clothing. The resources that are used to produce clothes and accessories — the materials, the energy, and the creative ideas that went into their making — are simply lost.

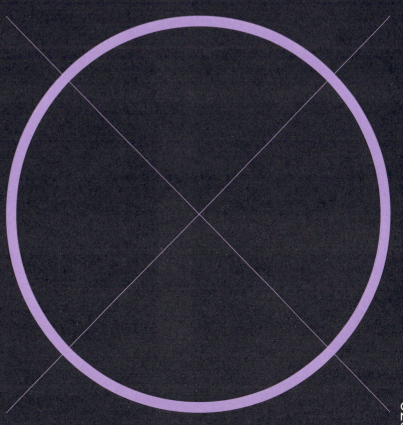

● Every year, the fashion industry is responsible for more greenhouse gas emissions than all international flights and container ships combined.[7] Through soil degradation, the use of natural ecosystems for raw material production, and waterway pollution, the industry is also a significant contributor to bio-diversity loss.[8]

● Textiles can release microfibres that end up in the ocean and freshwater.[9] These can be from synthetic fibres such as polyester, nylon, or acrylic that won't biodegrade, or from natural fibres whose coating or dyeing renders them non-biodegradable. Microfibres can transport toxic substances that are harmful if ingested by marine life. Some of the chemicals used in the dyeing and finishing process of clothes are known to be harmful to human health.[10]

CAN BE HARMFUL.

TODAY LESS THAN 1% OF CLOTHES ARE RECYCLED INTO NEW CLOTHES.

● This is due to clothing being created without considering its ability to be recycled, for example by using complex material blends or hard to separate components. This limits the incentives to invest in collection and recycling infrastructure, making high levels of recycling even more difficult to achieve.

WHILE LOCAL COMMUNITIES BENEFIT FROM EMPLOYMENT IN THE FASHION INDUSTRY, MANY SUFFER FROM ITS POOR PRACTICES.

● There are numerous examples of untreated wastewater from clothing production being discharged into local rivers, making water unsafe for drinking, bathing, or fishing.[11] In addition, cost and time pressures, unsafe processes, and the use of hazardous substances have led to poor and dangerous working conditions for many. Long hours and low pay are prevalent,[12] and instances of modern slavery and child labour have been reported.[13]

THERE IS NO DOUBT THAT THERE IS A NEED FOR POSITIVE CHANGE IN THE FASHION INDUSTRY.

FOR MANY, THE JOURNEY HAS ALREADY STARTED.

● Recent years have seen many brands and retailers taking action to be more sustainable, for example by reducing carbon emissions and water use. While these efforts are necessary, they too often simply focus on doing less bad within the confines of our current take-make-waste system. Doing less bad is important — but it's not enough. It merely delays disastrous outcomes. We need to move towards doing more good.

WE NEED
A SYSTEM
CHANGE.

WE NEED
A CIRCULAR
ECONOMY.

"Circular design is the *glue* that holds materials, design and business models together. It empowers designers and ignites change. It motivates creatives to look at products in an entirely different way and enables access to options beyond selecting organic or recycled materials."

Esther Verburg
EVP, Sustainable Business and Innovation
Tommy Hilfiger, owned by PVH Corp

CIRCULAR DESIGN COMBINES

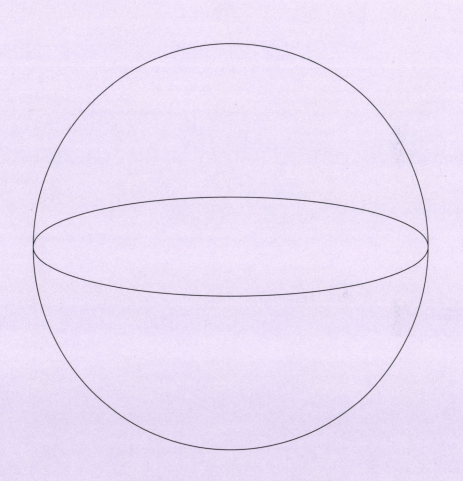

CIRCULAR ECONOMY PRINCIPLES AND SYSTEMS THINKING

Circular design has the power to expand our vision, boost our creativity, and create a more resilient and thriving fashion industry.

Circular design is a mission-led practice of design based on the principles of the circular economy and systems thinking.

The circular economy is a systems solution framework that empowers people to address global challenges, including climate change, biodiversity loss, waste, and pollution. It relies on three principles, all driven by design:

1. **Eliminate waste and pollution**
2. **Circulate products and materials**
3. **Regenerate nature**

In a circular economy, business models, products, and materials are designed to increase use and reuse, creating an economy in which nothing becomes waste and everything has value.

Increasingly based on renewable energy and materials, the circular economy is a resilient, distributed, diverse, and inclusive economic model. It is a bigger idea than addressing the symptoms of today's wasteful and polluting economy. It represents an opportunity to fundamentally redesign our economic model to benefit society, businesses, and the environment.

A circular economy begins with good design. It calls for a fresh approach to every decision made in the creation of fashion. It means not only designing the products of the future, but also the processes, services, businesses, and narratives that will deliver them. It leads to a change of mindset to proactively seek to make a positive impact, to shift from linear to circular, and to regenerate and restore by design.

The circular economy is accelerated by digital innovation. Digital technologies can unlock new opportunities in material innovation, enhance traceability and connectivity, and provide user-friendly platforms to access fashion.

Circular design has the power to expand our vision, boost our creativity, and create a more resilient and thriving fashion industry.

"From an intellectual point of view, circular design is fundamentally about seeing connections and designing in new patterns.

It is innovation in the context of the need to maximise the circulation, utilisation and iteration of apparel.

It is about designing collaborations within organisations, across functions, and sometimes building bridges to work in a precompetitive way across the industry to reimagine systems and implement them.

It is about organisations that are willing to try new things, experiment with different forms of abundance, and ask questions about how to grow in ways that also grow the pie for us all.

It is about design and creative spaces that allow for new thinking to emerge.

It is about having a vision for a circular operating system and working back from that.

It is about realising the potential of a more distributed, decentralised, and resilient business model.

"Business leaders are increasingly convinced of the *why*. Designers can show the pathway to the *how*."

Chris Grantham
Executive Director
Circular Economy
IDEO

THE WAY FORWARD

IS CIRCULAR

THREE MYTHS AND THREE TRUTHS ABOUT CIRCULAR DESIGN

"The biggest misconception about sustainability and circular design is that they are trends."

Kevin Germanier
Founder
Germanier

THREE MYTHS AND THREE TRUTHS ABOUT CIRCULAR DESIGN

Redesigning the future of fashion is a complex and ambitious challenge. But by debunking common misconceptions about circular design and diving into what it truly is, we can focus our efforts to achieve a circular economy for fashion.

MYTHS

PEOPLE THINK
IT IS ALL ABOUT
RECYCLING

046

PEOPLE THINK
IT IS ALL ABOUT
MAKING PRODUCTS
PHYSICALLY DURABLE

050

PEOPLE THINK
IT IS ALL ABOUT
PRODUCT
DESIGN

052

TRUTHS

IT IS AN
INTERDISCIPLINARY
AND
COLLABORATIVE
APPROACH

056

IT IS
AN ITERATIVE
PROCESS

060

IT IS
A JOURNEY

064

"When you appreciate how things are made, you then become more interested in knowing what will happen to those pieces during their lifetime."

Patrick McDowell
Founder and Designer
Patrick McDowell

MYTH 1

PEOPLE THINK IT IS ALL ABOUT RECYCLING

Designing products that are easily recyclable and made from recycled materials is an important part of circular design. But circular design is about much more than that. When we make something, we invest time, energy, and creativity into it, as well as materials. In a circular economy, the ambition is that none of this is wasted. That means not only thinking about a recycling loop but also other loops, such as reuse and remaking, that retain more of the product's original value.

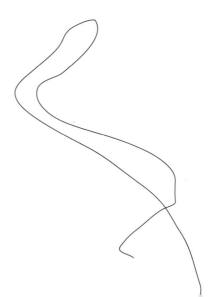

HARNESSING THE POWER OF THE INNER LOOPS

In a circular economy for fashion, the first priority for any product is to be used more and for longer. Once it cannot be used anymore, it can be remade into another product or its materials can be recycled. By making sure a product goes through the loops of sharing, longer use, reuse, and remaking before its materials are recycled or returned to nature, it is maintained at its highest value for as long as possible.

Designing clothes that are durable, easily repairable, and customisable means we can radically increase use, reducing cost per wear and lessening the environmental impact at the same time.

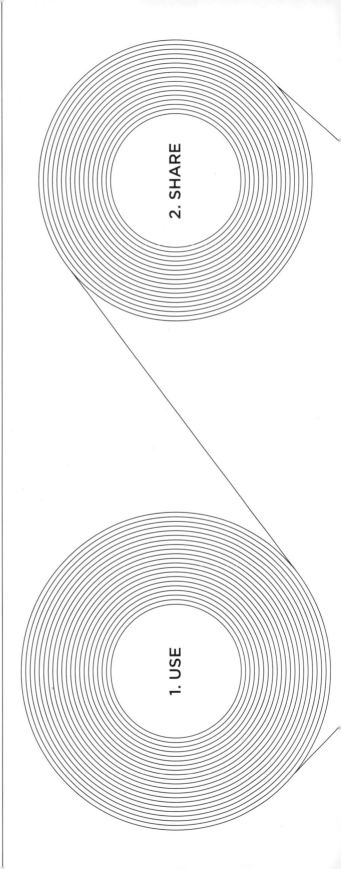

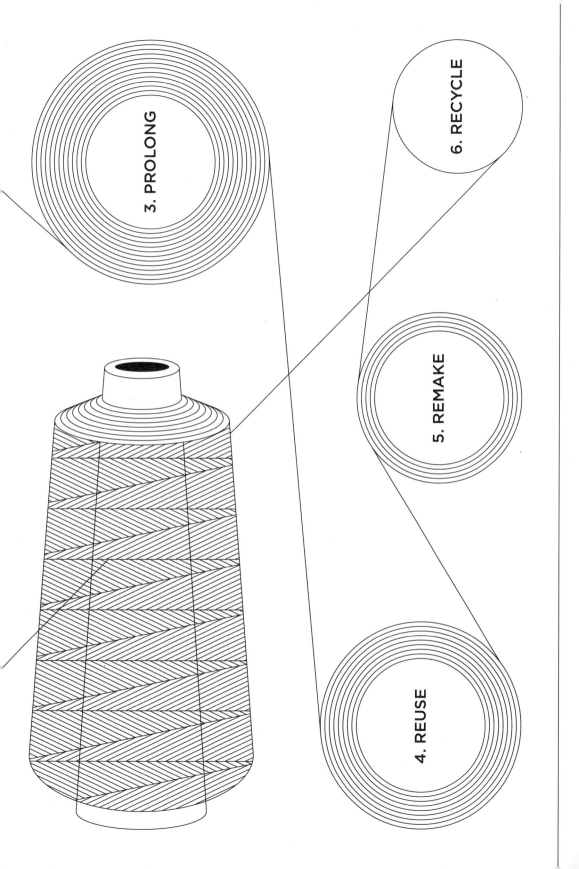

"Durability means developing clothes and accessories that keep intact the desire of customers to wear them, even years after having bought them."

Catherine Spindler
EVP Marketing and Branding
Lacoste

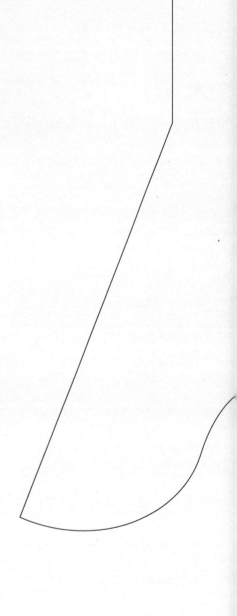

(MYTH 2)

PEOPLE THINK IT IS ALL ABOUT MAKING PRODUCTS PHYSICALLY DURABLE

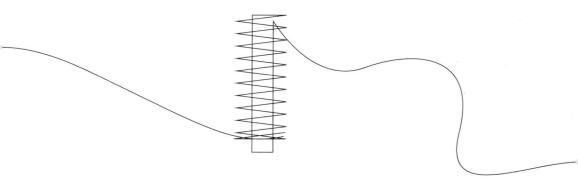

Emotional and physical durability go hand in hand and should be considered together in the circular design process.

When considering how to keep a product in use, often the first thing that comes to mind is how long it can be used before getting worn out: its physical durability. This is an important part of circular design, but it is not the only element that determines how long something will be used.

How long people will actually want to use a product, before it feels out of style for example, is as important to keep products in use. The emotional durability depends on a user valuing the product because of its timelessness, rarity, history, and meaning to them.

"In a circular design approach, the design stage is no longer a step in the value chain but an activity that takes place throughout the whole process."

Sergi Masip Sanz
Circular Economy Project Manager
Hallotex

MYTH 3

PEOPLE THINK IT IS ALL ABOUT PRODUCT DESIGN

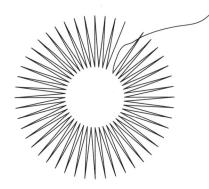

Circular design is about systems change.

When we think of design, the first things that come to mind are often items or structures, like a luxury gown. However, design also plays a pivotal role in creating the system that the gown is part of, the supply chain that is needed to make it, and the business model through which it reaches the person who will wear it. We might not even think of these things as *designed* because they are more abstract and have many architects. Yet people make decisions about how these systems work, and their decisions set in motion how we make, use, and reuse clothing and accessories.

Circular design therefore shapes not only the product composition, but also the system it fits into.

IT IS A
COLLAB-
ITERA
AND
ON
JOUR

BOUT
ORATION,
TION,
GOING
A
RNEY.

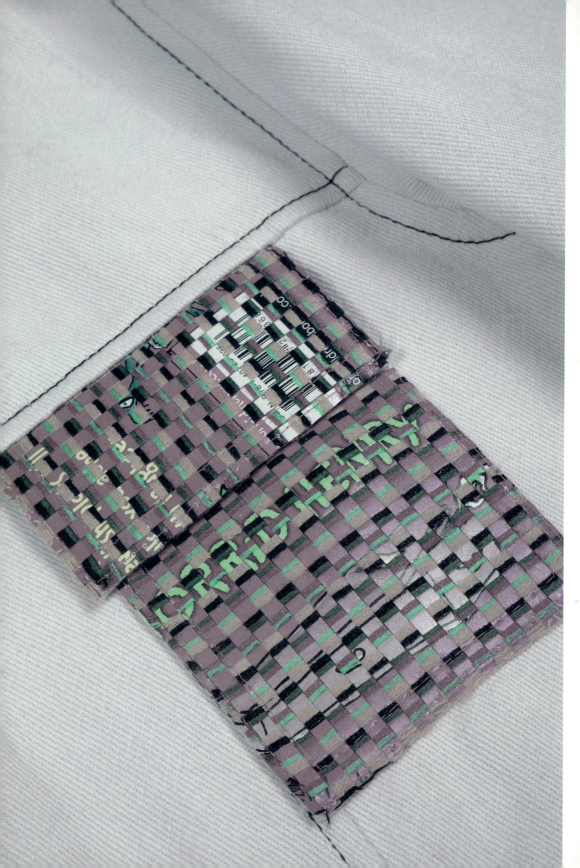

(TRUTH 1)

IT IS AN INTERDISCIPLINARY AND COLLABORATIVE APPROACH

Circular design is not only for people with *design* in their job title. The circular design process requires skills from across disciplines to make it a reality.

Elisabetta Baronio and an interdisciplinary team at VF Corporation, together with its partners, spent three years collaborating to create a jacket made from a single material that can be used and recycled forever, the Napapijri Circular Series jacket.

"Creativity is a community act."

Omoyemi Akerele
Founder and Executive Director
Style House Files
Lagos Fashion Week

CREATING TOGETHER

By

Elisabetta Baronio
Sustainability and CSR Manager
VF Corporation

The circular economy requires brands to change not just materials and business models but also the product creation flow. Prior to the Circular Series we could rely on an infinite set of fabrics, colours, and trims to choose from. After designing this jacket we learned how to deal with limitations, and we started to approach design in a completely different way.

The concept was simple: a jacket made entirely from a single material that could easily be recycled. But, as we thought more about it, the concept became more complex and we had to think beyond the usual design boundaries to consider a completely new business model. The rules and processes we were used to applying were not applicable in this case.

At first, we had design for disassembly in mind. We thought that was the most efficient and easiest way to approach circular design. But we soon faced the issue of the economic viability of recycling — who would ever want to recycle something that takes too much time to be divided into its different components? We realised that would be a problem.

Instead of starting from the idea, we had to start from the material. This decision required us to explore alternatives for each component and for each problem — we had to look for solutions to the material's limitations.

The design team could not do this alone. Circular design required us to go beyond our functional silos, to look at the product in a holistic way and understand that design is not all about aesthetics, shapes, and colours but about the entire product construction. It required a joint effort by several teams from within our organisation and across our supply chain. We engaged innovators, material scientists, designers, and sourcing teams.

Together, we worked within the limitations of current technology and found that the only synthetic material that could be recycled in a circular system was nylon 6. But we had to look beyond fabrics. What about the trims? If nylon 6 was the best fabric to use, could we find any zips on the market that were also made from 100% nylon 6? The answer was no, such a zip did not exist. We started to work closely with our suppliers to develop a zip made from nylon 6.

Then we did the same for the padding. We had to develop it from scratch, and it wasn't straightforward. We faced issues with the density of the padding, with the insulation capabilities. So, again, we had to involve suppliers and experts to create it.

Each of the 25 components of the jacket had to be made from nylon 6. As we went through them one by one, we realised that our brand's circular design effort had suddenly become an innovation project that would benefit the industry.

We reimagined everything in line with circular design, rethinking the very concept of creativity and the idea of infinite options to work with a finite set of options. The design of the jacket required educating entire teams about the technologies and options available on the market, as well as their limitations, creating discussions and fostering learning.

Once we had created the Circular Series jacket, we needed to explore options to make sure it was actually recycled and made into a new jacket in practice. We built a relationship with a partner, Aquafil, that tested the recyclability of the product and offered its technology to process the jacket once it reached the end of its usable life. We built a dedicated Infinity community in our organisation and created a digital take-back programme to ensure we could keep track of each jacket and enable customers to send it back to us. The jacket brought us to a new way of doing business.

It was evident that circular design needed to be thought into the system. We had to understand how the jacket would be used and the possible ways it could be returned to us so we could reuse its materials to make new products.

AS THE EXAMPLE OF
VF CORPORATION GOES TO SHOW:

- The challenge of moving towards a circular economy is too big to be tackled by any one company on its own. Collaboration across the industry, with organisations considered competitors or with suppliers, is necessary.
- Solving systemic issues requires interdisciplinary teams. For the Napapijri team, finding the best solution required a profound understanding of the system. This could only be achieved by a team with a broad range of expertise and skills.

(TRUTH 2)

IT IS AN ITERATIVE PROCESS

Transforming how clothes are designed and made cannot always be achieved in one go. Making progress means being open to imperfections in the process and to iterating and refining as you go along.

A collaboration between H&M, Bank & Vogue, and Renewcell to create the first dress made of Circulose®, a type of recycled cotton, shows the importance of iteration as part of the circular design process.

"Whenever I face a new ambitious and avant-garde project, I apply my progress-not-perfection idea, which allows me to make constant forward moves and overcome perfectionism blocks."

Marina Testino
Founder and Creative Director
Point Off View

ITERATING TOGETHER

By

Nellie Lindeborg
Sustainability Responsible
Assortment
H&M

Jasmine Qian
Research and Developer
H&M

Ella Soccorsi
Senior Designer
H&M

Harald Cavalli-Björkman
Chief Marketing Officer
Renewcell

Steven Bethell
President and Partner
Bank & Vogue

To create the Circulose® dress, we went through a number of iterations. We experimented, tested a lot, went back to the design table to correct things, and the result was a dress made with a fibre created using 50% of an old one.

Key to our ongoing partnership is the premise that we do not use clothes that can be worn again as they are. We only take what would otherwise end up in landfill. Our aim is to only design with what is available, without creating waste.

As feedstock for clothes is one of the biggest challenges facing the fashion industry, to be part of a design process that looks to overcome that challenge is really exciting. We had all been anticipating this new fibre and seeing Circulose® for the first time was impressive.

Working with Circulose® took many years and iterations because we needed to both consider what the user wanted and what quality of fabric we needed to achieve. The first batch of the fibre was made from old denim collected by Bank & Vogue. It was light blue because that was the colour of the original material, so we needed to design around that and, in the end, dyed it darker. Managing and testing the shrinkage took time through trial and error.

There is a big difference between doing something in the lab and doing something at scale — there are different skills you need to have. Once we got the technology to work, there were business challenges to overcome. For example, just connecting the collector and having a sorting plant where it would be most effective required a business case.

There are challenges to designing a product and system that is circular. It is pricey to sort textiles for recycling manually — a consequence of the industry moving towards more blended materials. However, automated processes to help with the sorting show a lot of promise and there are some interesting projects underway in this area, such as infrared scanning to identify and sort blends.

By testing the Circulose® dress with customers, we know there is a market for products like this. We reached our sales goals even in the midst of the COVID-19 pandemic. The dresses were almost sold out after only a few hours. People seemed to want to buy sustainable clothes despite everything being so uncertain. It shows what is important for many people.

We have been very grateful to be able to support each other through the initial design process. Everything took more iterations than with other projects. But in the end, all the people involved — across all levels of the supply chain that have worked on it — feel really proud of what we achieved together. Everyone loves the dress, and now we keep on moving forward!

AS THE EXAMPLE FROM H&M,
BANK & VOGUE, AND RENEWCELL
GOES TO SHOW:

- Creating feedback loops to learn, iterate, and improve over time is a fundamental part of the circular design approach. The scale of change can be intimidating, making learning along the way crucial.
- New and innovative practices take time to get right. A lot of unexpected challenges can arise when taking a solution from small to large scale. When adopting a circular design approach, there is value in allowing time and space to iterate solutions.

TRUTH 3

IT
IS
A
JOURNEY

Reshaping the fashion industry from linear to circular won't happen overnight. It is a journey of discovery that may start small but has endless possibilities.

In July 2019, a collaboration between the Ellen MacArthur Foundation and around 80 experts in the fashion industry led to the launch of *The Jeans Redesign* guidelines, a definition of jeans created in line with circular economy principles. The work built on existing efforts to improve jeans production, including C&A and Fashion For Good's open source guide *Developing Cradle to Cradle Certified™ Jeans*.

"The most important thing is to begin the journey, no matter how small the first steps may seem. Once an intention and commitment have been set, the forward momentum will lead to ongoing transformation."

Amber Olson Testino
Founder
Art Partner

STARTING ON
THE JOURNEY

By

Laura Balmond
Make Fashion Circular Lead
Ellen MacArthur Foundation

François Souchet
Former Make Fashion Circular Lead
Ellen MacArthur Foundation

Applying the high-level principles of the circular economy to fashion can seem like an overwhelming task. One of the questions we get asked time and time again is *where do we start?*

In 2019, we decided to pick one iconic item that many brands have in their collections to set an example of how companies can start their journey towards creating more circular products. We landed on jeans.

To be circular, the jeans would need to be both durable — so they could be worn for as long as possible — and recyclable. This is a tall order given the design choices that make jeans durable are often in conflict with those that make them recyclable. To better understand the issues, we spent time with a number of recyclers, all using different processes, to identify the current challenges around recycling 100% of the materials used.

They explained that the seams are often too thick to be shredded and the hardware and trims, such as buttons and rivets, require a lot of manual work to remove as they can't go through the shredding process. The recyclers explained their processes work best, both in terms of output quality and economic efficiency, when only one type of material is used. However, jeans are usually made from a mix of cotton, viscose, polyester, and elastane to provide strength and functionality.

As well as balancing durability with recyclability, our discussions with manufacturers and organisations, including ZDHC, revealed that changes would need to be made to eliminate waste and pollution in the jeans production process. While progress has been made to reduce the negative impacts of jeans production, hazardous chemicals are still widely used across the industry to create a worn look, even though they pose a risk to the workers who apply them and the environment. In addition, some of the processes, such as applying acid or stone washing, impact the product's durability.

After many conversations, one thing was clear: we needed to create alignment on *what good looks like* for all parts of the supply chain. So, in February 2019, we invited brands, retailers, manufacturers, recyclers, and NGOs to come to London for a design sprint. We spent almost two days together, sharing perspectives, challenges, and opportunities in each part of the value chain. We set out to not leave the room until we had an agreement on ambitious criteria for circular jeans that could be applied with today's technologies at scale. These were *The Jeans Redesign* Guidelines.

We didn't stop there. We brought together over 70 leading brands, manufacturers, and mills to put the guidelines into practice and bring jeans that aligned with the guidelines to the market. This practical element very quickly opened up collaborative conversations about how to achieve our common goal. By getting started without having perfect solutions in mind, all organisations involved experienced circular design first hand. Some trialled and found new ways of working that they will continue to use, some began to experiment with applying the principles to other products, and some established new collaborations.

Even after all this time and effort, we still haven't got all the answers on durability, materials innovation, or recycling technologies. We may even have more questions than when we started. Still, we now know we are asking the right questions, and in the absence of a perfect solution, we have started to move in the right direction. It's the beginning of an exciting journey. *The Jeans Redesign* has shown us what's possible, and all those who have already embarked with us on this journey are making it happen.

1 The jeans are collected and sorted by colour.
2 Components such as metal rivets, zippers, and other trims prevent the entire jean from being fully recycled. Certain pieces need to be cut off for the fabric to enter the recycling process.
3 Those pieces of fabric are mechanically shredded.
4 In order to be transformed into new yarn, the fibre goes through the shredding process several times.
5 Step by step, the fibre is spun into yarn.
6 Over time, the yarn becomes thinner and thinner.

REDESIGN WHAT GOOD JEANS LOOK LIKE

By

Michele Sizemore
Senior Vice-President
Global Product Development
Gap

Denim is at the heart of Gap, it's in our DNA, this is our sweet spot. Yet, there are so many roadblocks in the day-to-day development of our products that it can sometimes prevent us from being as innovative as we'd like. What we did through *The Jeans Redesign* project was set those issues aside, taking the shackles off. We focused on what we wanted to achieve, setting clear parameters to solve for circularity, going beyond previous sustainability ambitions to find a solution.

While this work started with a small collection, it is fuelling something much bigger. It's a system change for us, and this is the start of the journey. We have to transform this industry. Through solving for jeans, we have learned and have been able to apply the principles to other products in our line, including our Generation Good collection as well. It's infectious in the best of ways. Our customers also want to participate, we just need to communicate it in a language they understand, and they're here for it.

Challenges that are this big call for industry-wide system-based solutions, and we don't believe we can do it alone. We need to work together with our peers across the fashion value chain to create solutions for a circular economy that are truly end-to-end and round again. That means not just engaging our designers but also those in our supplier base and vendors and even our competitors. That's why we love this project. Here we are with other retailers, normally our competitors, all in it together.

We have a responsibility and accountability to take part in this, and we can become a collective force for change.

MAKE THEM FIT FOR A CIRCULAR ECONOMY

By

Piyumi Perera
Head of Design
Hirdaramani Discovery Lab

Since we started working on *The Jeans Redesign* project two years ago, we've already come a long way. We began by looking at material health, and our journey into that has moved us to source differently. We make sure the fabric we're sourcing fits with the criteria to make our jeans part of a circular economy — that they have a percentage of recycled fibre in them and can be recycled when they can't be worn anymore.

Initially, it was difficult to find suppliers that were working with recycled fibres, and it was challenging for us to trace where the fibres had come from. The hardware on the jeans was another area we needed to re-evaluate. The first round of designing jeans that fit the guidelines was difficult but then it became progressively easier. Our designers became more and more comfortable with the criteria, and now it works really well. It's part of what we do.

Another challenge has been building partnerships in which we're all focused on creating jeans that are circular. On the other hand, when we've taken jeans designed with the guidelines to brands, it feels like we've been able to inspire them to work in similar ways. They might not call it circular, it might have a different name, but there's been a shift in how they're thinking and that's a step in the right direction. Whether we're working together directly or not, each development we make is changing the industry for the better. We're on the same journey.

7   The yarn is ready to be woven into new denim fabric.
8   The traditional dyeing process for denim requires a huge amount of water.
9   Some alternatives exist to use less to no water, but are still not available at scale.

ENSURE THEY NEVER BECOME WASTE

By

Paul Doertenbach
Managing Director
I:Collect GmbH

The way clothes are designed from the start is critical to how effectively and efficiently they can be collected, sorted, reused, and recycled. People across the whole industry need to get behind the idea of circular economy and make long-term efforts to make it work in fashion.
    Our mission at I:CO is to enable circular supply chains in the fashion industry. We want to pave the way for a critical mass of circular products to be collected and recycled through our take-back system. We hope that more brands and retailers will think of this as a vital part of their supply chains and start designing their jeans according to *The Jeans Redesign* Guidelines.
    The hope is that, in the future, all jeans will be made in a way that makes it possible for them to be reused and recycled. The more people are involved in the process, the better it becomes.

AS THE JEANS REDESIGN GOES TO SHOW:

o   Working towards a shared vision requires ambition but also an acceptance that solutions might not be perfect the first time around. The path will reveal new challenges, as well as exciting opportunities that are waiting to be unlocked. By embarking on the journey together, each organisation can benefit from the learnings of others and more quickly reach the shared goal.

10 Treating the water used for dyeing denim is key to avoid polluting water streams.
11 Through a very specific chemical process, the water used for dyeing treatment can return to a quality level that allows for safe return to the water streams.

THE JEANS REDESIGN

THESE JEANS WERE CREATED USING THE JEANS REDESIGN GUIDELINES, AN INITIATIVE THAT ENSURES WE W[ORK] TOGETHER AS AN INDUSTRY TO C[REATE] CIRCULAR AND DURABLE DENIM

THE DENIM YOU LOVE, MADE MORE SUSTAINABLE

BY CREATING DENIM THAT USES INNOVATIVE MATERIALS AND PROCESSING, WE'RE LOWERING OUR IMPACT ON THE ENVIRONMENT.

LEARN MORE ON **TOMMY.COM**

WASH LESS, INSIDE OUT, ON A COLD SETTING AND LINE DRY. REPAIR, DONATE OR RECYCLE **WASTE NOTHING, WELCOME ALL.**

JEANS TODAY

① WASTEFUL

○ Once a symbol of durable workwear, jeans are no longer designed to last for years. In addition, the way jeans are made, including the way fabric is constructed and chosen, rarely considers the amount of time they can be used or the recyclability of the materials once they are no longer in use.

○ Multiple material blends in the fabric

Denim fabric was traditionally made from cotton, but the desire for stretch denim, and its success, have led to an increase in blending cotton with plastic-based fibres, such as elastane. This mix of fibres presents a major obstacle to recycling used denim fabric into new fabric due to the limitations of current recycling technologies.

○ Rivets and trims

Metal rivets are difficult for recyclers to remove. As a consequence, for jeans today, large parts of the upper fabric of jeans are cut off and landfilled or incinerated.

② POLLUTING

○ Harmful substances and processes

Dyes and other chemicals used for finishing, as well as processes such as stone-washing and electroplating can have adverse effects on people and the environment. Some of the chemicals used can persist in the environment and may accumulate over time.[14]

After production, harmful substances often remain in textiles, both intentionally and unintentionally, and can cause harm to people handling or wearing them.[15]

VS
REDESIGNED JEANS

① DURABLE AND MADE TO LAST

○ Designing and producing jeans that last longer and offering them through business models that increase their use and help keep them in use and out of landfills and incinerators.

○ Physical durability

Jeans are designed to withstand a minimum of 30 home laundries and still meet the usual durability requirements of new jeans.

○ Care guide

Information is given to the customers to help them take care of their jeans, so they can use them more and longer.

② MADE FROM RECYCLABLE MATERIALS AND COMPONENTS

○ Mono-materials

All the fabrics used to make jeans are made from 98% cellulose-based fibres, by weight. This ensures the choice of materials aligns with available recycling technology so that it can practically be recycled after use. Post-consumer recycled content is also used in the composition of the jeans to help decouple from finite feedstocks and stimulate demand for collection and recycling.

○ Disassemblable components

Buttons, zips, and other components are designed for easy disassembly, enabling all components added to the fabric to be reused or recycled.

○ Rivets eliminated

Metal rivets are reduced or, ideally, eliminated so jeans can be easily recycled. Alternatives, such as bar tacks, are used instead.

③ HEALTHY INPUTS

○ Regenerative cotton

The cotton used for jeans is grown using regenerative farming methods (or organic or in transition methods in the shorter term).

○ Harmful chemicals eliminated

Chemicals used in production processes are safe and the following chemicals or processes are prohibited: conventional electroplating, potassium permanganate, sand blasting, stone finishing.

④ TRACEABILITY

○ Labelled for reuse, remaking, and recycling

Jeans are labelled so they are sorted and sent for reuse, remaking, or recycling, as appropriate. This information may also be made available to the sorter via technologies incorporated into the garment such as RFID, QR codes, and traceable fibre technology.

ADEBAYO
OKE-LAWAL

"Circular design is a state of creating a cycle that doesn't just take from a place but also contributes to it."

I founded Orange Culture in 2010. We are based in Nigeria and we run 90% of our activities here for a simple reason: for us circular design is a state of creating a cycle that doesn't just take from a place but also contributes to it.

We started with just one sewing machine and one tailor. At first, we had no distribution and very small scale production. Over the years and as the brand started to grow, I learnt a lot of things about Nigeria and its resources, and, step by step, we were able to set up a supply chain that is 90% local. We design, produce, dye, print, and even try to grow our cotton here!

Most importantly, what I want to show with Orange Culture is that the place you are taking your resources from doesn't have to suffer. Both the community and the environment can benefit from your work.

By keeping our supply chain local, we ensure that the money stays within the local communities. It also gives us the opportunity to train and educate our staff and suppliers about innovative ways to ensure the end product is not causing harm, waste, or pollution and we are not contributing to the problems in our environment.

This is our vision for a circular fashion industry: we want to contribute more than we take for the environment and the local communities.

DURAN LANTINK

"To me, it is natural to source the material I need to create beautiful clothes from materials that already exist. It actually sparks my creativity."

To me, it is natural to source the material I need to create beautiful clothes from materials that already exist. It actually sparks my creativity. My whole life, I have been designing this way but only recently identified as a circular designer.

When I was nominated for the LVMH Prize, I got tagged as an *upcycler* because I was using deadstock material to create my designs but it's about so much more than that. It's about making something old lovable again. I'm pushing the idea further as I also don't want my designs to be dependent on deadstock. Now, I am also asking my own customers to bring their clothes back to me so I can rebuild and restyle them. It is great because this way my customers keep an item that they already love and have a story and emotional connection with, but they also get this *newness* feeling with the restyling. It is also a great way to source materials locally as they come directly from customers' wardrobes.

As my brand grows and my collections are present in global cities, I also want to train local tailors, showing them my way to restyle garments. That way, my brand's entire supply can remain local from sourcing to production to retail, empowering local communities. I have been running a training programme in South Africa with marginalised trans people, showing them how to tailor, with this goal in mind.

"There is the classic idea of what a designer is or does: drawing something on a blank paper – tabula rasa – from one or another divine, immaterial source of inspiration. This was always a typical linear myth, and a fairly powerful one.

This linear concept of design is untenable, however, under any circular model. The designer's key task, creatively, becomes precisely not to create something new from immaterial inspirations but to forge connections with her already-existing material surrounding. We are to redefine design as being about transformation, hybridisation, and metamorphosis, departing from pre-existing products, matters, things, or materials. [16]"

Pepijn van Eeden
Former Chief Executive Officer
MARINE SERRE

3

DESIGNING USING SYSTEMS THINKING

"A system needs to
be understood before
it can be changed."

Noémie Balmat
Founder and CEO
Month Day Year

WHAT IS SYSTEMS THINKING?	084
REDESIGNING SUPPLY CHAINS, NOT JUST PRODUCTS	087
DESIGNING WITH PEOPLE AND FOR PEOPLE	093

DESIGNING USING SYSTEMS THINKING

Systems thinking, applied in concert with the principles of the circular economy, offers an approach to better understand the issues at stake in the fashion industry. It helps address complex problems, creates impact on a greater scale, and unlocks the true potential of a circular economy for fashion.

WHAT IS SYSTEMS THINKING?

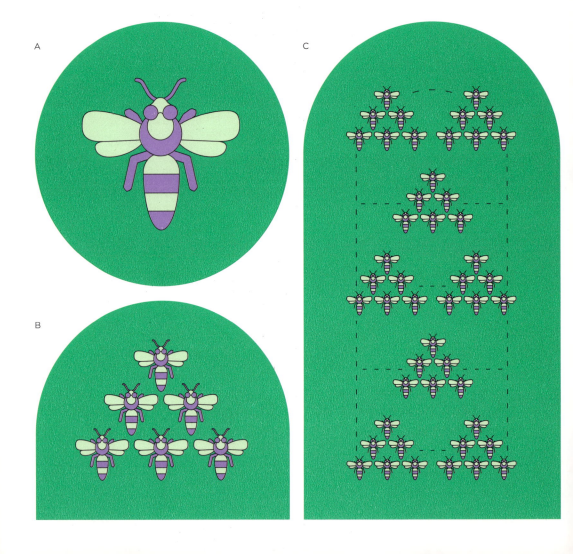

A

B

C

When we design something, there are many things we take into account: what our design will look like, how it's going to be used, and who is going to use it, for example. We first zoom in on the user.

User[A]

The user we zoom in on doesn't exist in isolation — they live within a context, a specific place in the world made of individual stories and relationships. For our designs to work in a circular economy, we need to zoom out and consider the context surrounding the users of our designs.

Context[B]

The context our user lives in has many layers: economic, environmental, and social. This context involves organisations, people, and processes. These systems are nested, interconnected and interdependent. Therefore, focusing on only one piece of a multifaceted picture can lead to a complex web of problems like the one we see in the fashion industry today.

To overcome these challenges, circular design places both the user and the context at the centre of the design process, designing for and within a wider system. This is where systems thinking comes in.

Systems[C]

Systems thinking means that, at every stage in the design process, we move back and forth between the user's needs and system awareness. We zoom in on the user's needs and zoom out to consider the implications on systems, oscillating continuously between these two equally critical perspectives. By zooming out and looking at the interconnections between the different parts of the system and understanding how every piece of the puzzle relates to the other, we can design a solution that positively impacts the system overall — not only meeting the user's needs but also providing environmental, social, and economic benefits.

Building this into the creative process breaks the illusion that we are just designing for one person or user. It uncloaks the complexity of the world around us and reveals how the challenges we aim to address are interrelated and constantly evolving. As such, designing for a circular economy requires acknowledging and embracing this complexity.

Based on his decades-long supply chain expertise, Bill McRaith, former Chief Supply Chain Officer at PVH Corp, which owns brands like Calvin Klein and Tommy Hilfiger, illustrates what it means to take a systems thinking approach and exposes the profound transformation opportunities for the global fashion system.

REDESIGNING SUPPLY CHAINS, NOT JUST PRODUCTS

By

Bill McRaith
Former Chief Supply Chain Officer
PVH Corp

Thinking about where you'd like your business to be in five years and how to get there? Then you need to be thinking about a lot more than just product, product design, or how to better engage the customer in a post-pandemic world. You have to already be addressing your business and supply chain operations if your ambitions are to become reality.

Today's supply chains were designed and built 10 to 20 years ago for a retail reality that no longer exists. They were often designed for predictable, one-way flows, where we told customers what they should buy. They were built to minimise the production cost of an individual item, rather than optimize a programme's profitability. Addressing unrealised profits due to stock-outs, markdowns, returns and damages was often given less effort than saving a few cents on product cost.

Now, the landscape of fashion and retail is increasingly dynamic. As customers and influencers have evolved to be drivers of fashion and ecommerce has boomed, the supply chains of yesterday no longer meet all of today's needs — let alone deliver on the circular fashion industry of tomorrow.

In order to address the customers' needs, eliminate purchasing waste, and start the work of truly building circular supply models, the first step is to stop thinking of supply as a chain. It is a lattice, or a matrix, dynamically adjusting and responding across off-shore, near-shore, and on-shore collaborative supply platforms.

To create a circular fashion industry, we need to ask ourselves the right questions to create the supply capability needed for tomorrow. If we want to eliminate waste, reduce our carbon footprint, and better respond to customers' needs by moving to on-demand manufacturing, for example, how are we going to do that? If an order is placed in the UK, we can't make it on demand in Asia as the time to market would simply be too long, at least if we are going to eliminate air freight, and you can't claim to be sustainable and then use air freight as a part of your speed model. And what if we're going to scale garment repair and recycling? It means thinking about supply from a global, regional, and local perspective, building a supply mesh that is truly collaborative rather than transactional.

When I envision the future of our supply environment at PVH, I see us in pre-competitive partnerships with other brands, manufacturers, advanced machine manufacturers, governments, and special interest groups. We are serious about our desire to drive fashion forward for good. We know that individually we can *do good* but collectively we can *do great*. Imagine a world where we are working with small, green and highly responsive manufacturing hubs across continents, with local repair service providers, new mass garment recycling centres that see waste as just another commodity, seamlessly integrating recycled materials into new garments, enabling our clothing to be circulated through new business models.

For some, it might seem impossible that supply could ever look fundamentally different from what it looks like today. Yet, I've personally experienced how quickly global transformations can happen. When I started my career in the UK, there was no *Made in Asia*, everything was made in the UK. When I moved to China 31 years ago there was virtually no export-oriented manufacturing and certainly no raw material or trim supply, except for the most basic materials. But over the last 30 years, Chinese manufacturing has come to represent a significant proportion of the global market. Many early movers helped shape that journey. There were many different perspectives on how China would be able to make goods that could compete with the quality of goods made in the UK, EU, and US. Today, the idea that people would have once questioned China or Asia's capability is incomprehensible.

In the next 15 years, we can and will, once again, transform global supply chains. We have the opportunity to learn from the past, take stock of all the things we wish we'd done better, and build a more resilient, dynamic, effective, circular supply network. There's never been a more opportune moment to change the game.

"There's never been a more opportune moment to change the game."

Bill McRaith
Former Chief Supply Chain Officer
PVH Corp

"We need to think about how a circular economy can benefit society, as any changes to the structure of the economy will affect social systems too. If we fail to see the economic, social, and environmental spheres as intimately connected, we will miss the point – the vitality of one affects the vitality of them all."

Josie Warden
Associate Director
RSA

DESIGNING WITH PEOPLE AND FOR PEOPLE

Systems thinking helps us understand the complexity of supply chains and customer relationships and recognise the impacts of our activities on society.
      Many creatives already appreciate that their actions have ripple effects throughout the wider system and have started on a journey to design with and for people. This means thinking about the wellbeing of all people across the fashion supply chain, as well as the diversity of the communities we create for. The stories in this chapter demonstrate the abundance of ways to create positive impact, far beyond a single product, range, or season.

DESIGNING
WITH PEOPLE

Creatives are already exploring solutions to empower and ensure the fair and equal treatment of everyone involved in making their products.

Designers, producers, and users of clothes are deeply connected. We don't bring products and services to life by ourselves: a huge number of people are involved in making what we conceive into a reality. Despite this, cost, time pressures, and unsafe processes have often harmed those working in the fashion industry. This has a human cost, creates fragility in the supply chain, and is under increasing scrutiny from the media and public. By contrast, working to create healthy, thriving communities will not only improve many people's lives but also increase the resilience of the overall system.

"Previously, designers didn't have to think about the source of the materials, the labour associated with production or the sales channels to get the product to the customer – that was someone else's role. By understanding other functions in the supply chain and how design contributes to each, we will create a new approach that is more inclusive, empathetic and agile."

Kristen Nuttall
Senior Designer Sustainability
adidas

BETHANY WILLIAMS

DESIGNER BETHANY WILLIAMS

links each of her collections to a charitable cause.

Her collections are manufactured

through a network of social projects.

From Making for Change, a fashion training and manufacturing unit within HMP Downview women's prison in the UK, to San Patrignano, an Italian organisation that welcomes those suffering from drug addiction and marginalisation,

Bethany has created a whole system in which each organisation helps others thrive.

NIGERIA-BASED BRAND ORANGE CULTURE

tries to source and produce locally so that the local community can benefit from its work, not only in economic terms

but also by empowering local communities with specific savoir-faire and training.

TECHNOLOGY PLATFORM POWERED BY PEOPLE

enables distributed manufacturing where small-scale producers and artisans around the world are connected

with large international brands and retail buyers, driving better growth in local communities, reducing inventory, and increasing efficiencies along the supply chain.

POWERED BY PEOPLE

ORANGE CULTURE

DESIGNER
DURAN LANTINK

takes unsold stock

and turns it into entirely new garments

to be sold in the same place where the originals were collected.

In line with recreating new garments using only local sources,

employing local tailors who are trained to recreate beautiful pieces out of old ones is also a priority.

BRAZILIAN AGROFORESTRY INITIATIVE
FARFARM

works with farmers and trains them

in agroforestry and intercropping practices.

This way, farmers can earn multiple revenue streams

from cash crops for the food, fashion, and beauty industries,

leading to higher incomes and greater resilience.

DURAN LANTINK

DESIGNING
FOR
PEOPLE

Creatives are already exploring solutions for inclusive designs that serve everyone.

Whether we are creating a shirt or a shopping experience, when we design products and services for the fashion industry, we want people to use and enjoy them. It is in our interest to shape a fashion system that is distributed, diverse, and inclusive, as it offers new ways for more people to participate.

Inclusive design ensures the needs and preferences of everyone in the population are met.[17] This requires a strong understanding of user diversity from a race, gender, socio-economic, and physical perspective.[18] Allowing everybody to find fashion items that cater to their needs enables us all to express ourselves through clothing. As well as increasing access to garments, this approach can encourage their reuse. Designing pieces that are genderfluid, one size fits all, or unisex can, for example, help ensure they are kept in use for longer since they can be worn by many different people.

"We are old, young, live with disability and difficulties, and speak multiple languages; we are diverse individuals and communities. However, often goods and services are designed as if we are all the same. Design that embraces diversity maximises widespread access and usability, meaning more people are included. Both individuals and organisations benefit from making inclusive design a standard practice."

PwC Australia and Centre for Inclusive Design
The Benefits of Designing for Everyone (2019)

GOOD AMERICAN

GOOD AMERICAN

Was founded in October 2016 by Emma Grede and Khloé Kardashian.

It is an inclusive fashion brand that offers trend-forward designs made to fit women of all sizes.

Since its inception, the brand has provided high-quality denim

and expanded to new categories in sizes 00–32, as well as introducing collections catered to accentuate women's curves

with designs such as *Good Waist* and *Good Legs*.

LIFESTYLE AND ACCESSORIES BRAND FFORA

designs accessories for wheelchair users,

a community of people

whose needs and perspectives

are seldom catered for

in the fashion industry.

FFORA

PROCLAIM

UNDERWEAR COMPANY PROCLAIM

TAKAFUMI TSURUTA

makes sure its products are inclusive

and designed for all skin tones.

The brand is founded on the principles

that fashion should represent all women

and can be made in a way that does good for people and the planet.[19]

focuses most of his designs

on their ability to fit as many people with disabilities as possible.

His collection goes beyond pure practicality,

as he defines disability as a source of empowerment. This is illustrated most notably in his dress that uses a braille pattern instead of traditional polka dot.[20] He has also created a dress to help YKK, a top brand in the worldwide fastening market,

meet its goal to design a universal design zipper.

TAKAFUMI TSURUTA

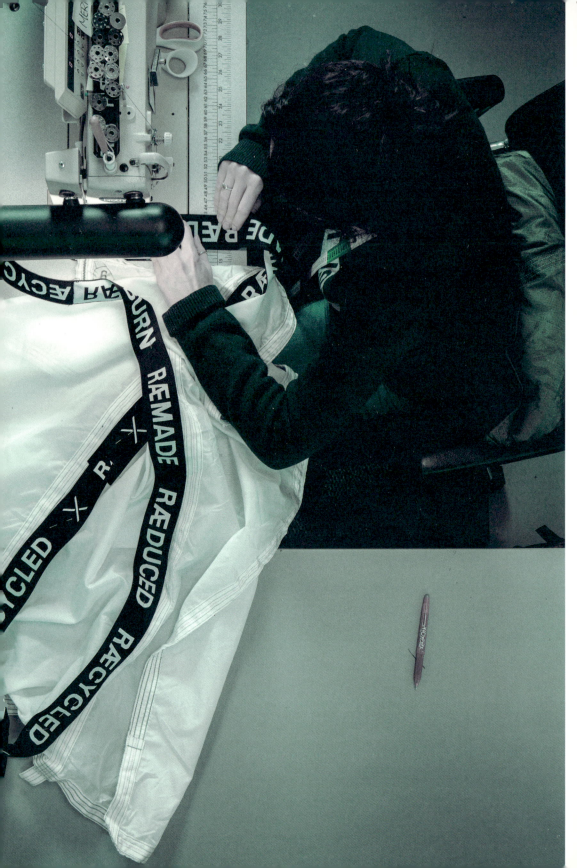

4

DESIGNING WITH THREE PRINCIPLES IN MIND

THIS CHAPTER COVERS 15 STRATEGIES THAT CREATIVES ARE ALREADY EXPLORING TODAY.

1	ELIMINATE WASTE AND POLLUTION	A.	Wear bits, not atoms	122
		B.	Make what you sell	124
		C.	Use safe, recycled, renewable materials	126
		D.	Create zero manufacturing waste	130
2	CIRCULATE PRODUCTS AND MATERIALS	E.	Make fashion that lasts	142
		F.	Reconnect people and clothing	144
		G.	Take back and repair	146
		H.	Use data for durability	148
		I.	Create an online wardrobe	150
		J.	Pass products from one user to the next	152
		K.	Remake and restyle	154
		L.	Use what you have	156
		M.	Make to be made again	158
		N.	Make information available	160
3	REGENERATE NATURE	O.	Regenerative as well as renewable	170

DESIGNING WITH THREE PRINCIPLES IN MIND

For design and creative professionals, these three principles act as a goal. They help us evaluate whether our creations support the shift to a circular economy or keep us within the frustrations and limitations of today's linear economy.

This section acts as a reference guide, enabling you to explore numerous design strategies for each of the three principles, with case examples and insights from contemporary pioneers who have applied this thinking in their work.

As you explore the strategies in this chapter, keep in mind that the potential of circular design goes beyond viewing or deploying them in isolation. Simply prioritising durability, sharing, or renewable materials alone, for example, would miss the opportunity that the circular economy presents.

The greater opportunity is to view these strategies in the bigger picture, understand how they are complementary, and combine those that are relevant in your specific context.

THE BUTTERFLY DIAGRAM OF A 100% COTTON T-SHIRT

The three principles are illustrated in *the butterfly diagram*, which shows how different materials can flow between two cycles. It's best brought to life through an example.

1 Cotton begins its life on the left antenna of the butterfly. If it is grown regeneratively — safeguarding the health of the soil and surrounding ecosystem — it can be produced time and time again with a little help from the sun, water, and nutrients in the soil. Grown this way, it can be a renewable resource.

2 Once harvested from the field, the cotton is processed and spun into yarn, woven into fabric, and cut and sewn. It travels down the body of the butterfly to become a T-shirt, before ending up in the hands of a user. In the linear economy, the cotton T-shirt would then drop off the diagram, ending up in landfill or incineration after use.

3 However, in the circular economy the cotton T-shirt goes on a journey through loops that maintain the value of the T-shirt and the materials it is made from — the wings of the butterfly.

It begins on the right-hand side, going through *technical cycles* that keep it at its highest value, retaining the energy, labour, and time invested during production. The cotton T-shirt is worn time and time again by one or many people. It is repaired when it becomes damaged so it can keep being worn. And, when it can no longer be fixed, it is recycled into a new cotton fibre, ready to travel back down the body of the butterfly and become a new product.

4 When the cotton is no longer able to be recycled to a standard where it can be spun into new yarn, it makes its way to the left wing of the butterfly, the biological cycle. This can happen only if the cotton has not been treated with hazardous dyes or chemicals during its many technical cycles, because when the cotton moves to the left wing of the butterfly, it is composted and returned to the soil it came from. There, it contributes to the growth of new crops, perhaps cotton, ready to start the journey through the circular economy.

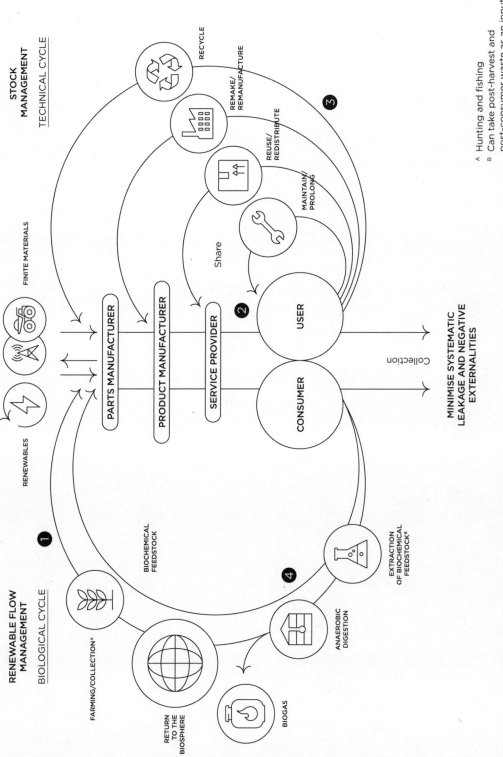

①

"It is essential to understand that we cannot create new products without also acting on the waste and pollution linked to them."

Costanza Lombardi
Former Buyer Women's RTW
Browns

ELIMINATE WASTE AND POLLUTION

Waste and pollution are the consequences of decisions made at the design stage. By viewing waste and pollution as design flaws, we can change our perspective on what we are designing. Rather than cleaning up the problem later on, how might we eliminate waste and pollution from the start?

There are many ways to eliminate waste and pollution from the fashion industry through circular design.
　　　　　This chapter covers four strategies that creatives are already exploring to eliminate waste and pollution.
　　　　　Eliminating waste and pollution does not end with these strategies. The creative possibilities are endless, and these models can be built on in the future.

ICICLE

By
Tao Xiaoma
Ye Shouzeng

"Circular design goes way beyond recycling. It is a philosophy, a state of mind that accompanies us in every design decision."

My husband and I founded Icicle in 1997. After studying fashion design at Donghua University in Shanghai, we decided to establish a brand inspired by the traditional Chinese philosophy of the harmony between humans and nature, a wisdom that has sustained the Chinese way of living and thinking for thousands of years.

Based on this philosophy, we decided to follow three interdependent principles: respect nature (敬天), be kind to others (爱人) and cherish what is given to us (惜物). These three principles build up what we call the Natural Way, and as a brand, we decided to focus our work on pursuing the Natural Way of Living through the Natural Way of Creating and Producing.

To respect nature means that we seek a reciprocal relationship between us and nature. We understand that nature is the ultimate source of our creation and in return we must protect it. This is why we use natural materials like cashmere, linen, wool, silk, and cotton that are dyed with natural plant dyes or are left in natural colours. We help our customers engage with the beauty of those natural materials made with minimised human intervention.

We focus our designs on minimalistic, trend-less, and durable pieces that our customers can wear for a long time and use on many different occasions.

To us, circular design goes way beyond recycling. It is a philosophy, a state of mind that accompanies us in every design decision.

NKWO ONWUKA

When I moved back to Nigeria from the UK in 2016, one of my favourite places to visit became the craft markets. I spoke to weavers, fabric dyers, even people casting bronze, and soon I realised two things: one was the difficulty those artisans had in sourcing good quality materials to work with and the other thing was that many of them were the last in their line of craft.

Nigeria has a lot of second-hand markets and a strong culture of clothing being made by small-scale manufacturers, dressmakers, and independent designers. We also have a very active social life here. We love to celebrate and get dressed up with weddings, parties, and church events going on every weekend. The result of all this is piles and piles of textile waste.

Looking at those piles, I started to explore and experiment. How could I prevent offcuts, deadstock fabrics, and old clothes from ending up in landfill or being incinerated? How could I use them as raw material, at the same time as preserving our traditional handicraft skills?

It was in looking for a way to come up with a more intentional and permanent solution to achieve zero waste that I invented a new African textile called DAKALA CLOTH with an innovative technique of stripping and sewing.

I am currently working with weavers on traditional hand looms to add another dimension to this textile waste cloth so it can be scaled up. Through preserving this wonderful age-old craft, we are weaving waste into wealth.

"Through preserving this wonderful age-old craft, we are weaving waste into wealth."

GABRIELA HEARST

"Waste is a design flaw as it doesn't exist in nature."

I grew up in a circular system. My family's 170-year-old farm, where my mother still lives, is off the grid. You can breed or grow as much as the land allows. Nothing goes to waste, things are intended to last, quality is a utilitarian aspect. This experience informed the two main values Gabriela Hearst is built on: a long-term view and sustainability. Sustainability is about eliminating waste. Waste is a design flaw as it doesn't exist in nature. We consider waste and the impact on the environment in every choice we make, from design to business strategy. For our first show in 2017, we made 30% of our collection from deadstock fabrics. This number has increased to 60% for our most recent Resort collection, while our men's line only uses repurposed materials. In 2019, we achieved the goal of being plastic-free, both front and back of house, using compostable packaging and recycled cardboard hangers. We opened stores that are designed and built in an environmentally conscious way: we made sure 90% of the material waste generated during construction was recycled. We were the first fashion company to start measuring the carbon footprint of our fashion show and offsetting it — a practice that has become an industry standard. Our commitment to create the highest quality products with the lowest impact on the environment is the driving force behind Gabriela Hearst. If we stop evolving in this commitment, we stop evolving as a company. It is our own beating heart.

A. **Wear bits, not atoms**

How might we deliver fashion products and experiences without the need to produce clothes?

"What could be more radical than making nothing at all?"

Christopher Raeburn
Creative Director
RÆBURN and Timberland

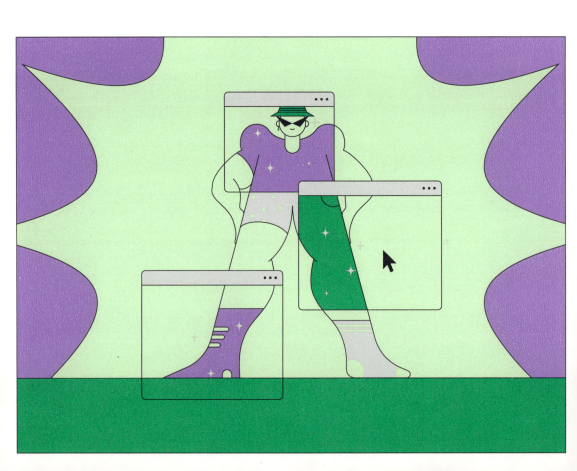

Why?	User needs can sometimes be met without creating a physical product. During the COVID-19 pandemic, rapid digital transformation highlighted opportunities for virtual fashion, from online fashion shows and fashion films to virtual clothing ready for digital wear.
What?	Fashion items or collections are designed and delivered digitally and are then used for online digital wear. Users can purchase digital garments, fit them onto a picture of themselves or an avatar, and then share this content across their social media platforms. In the same way, brands can present their collections using virtual models, which can be avatars of original models or completely new characters. Fashion shows or experiences can also be delivered through a combination of real and virtual environments, thus scaling their reach and limiting travel for attendees. Technologies such as augmented and virtual reality offer the opportunity to enjoy the shows from any location and virtually try on garments in a digital shopping journey.
Who is pioneering it?	○ Scandinavian multi-brand retailer Carlings launched its first virtual collection in November 2018. It sold out in under a week at a cost of EUR 10 to EUR 30 (roughly USD 11 to USD 34) per piece.[21] Customers supplied a photo that designers at Carlings manipulated so it appeared they were dressed in the apparel. ○ The Diigitals is a digital-only model agency created by Cameron-James Wilson, a fashion photographer turned 3D artist. The Diigitals now holds a portfolio of seven digital models. It all started in 2017 when Cameron designed Shudu, the first digital supermodel, and launched its Instagram page. Since then, Shudu has modelled for brands from Ferragamo to Louboutin and been featured in fashion magazines including *Vogue*, *Harper's Bazaar*, and *GQ*. ○ DressX allows users to purchase digital fashion. Users can acquire digital looks by uploading their photo to DressX and choosing the garment they want to digitally wear. They then receive the picture of themselves with the selected look, which can be shared on social media or used to curate their own virtual identities. ○ The Fabricant is a digital fashion house that collaborates with physical brands such as Puma, Off-White, and Tommy Hilfiger to create digital marketing campaigns and collections. It also creates its own digital-only couture pieces, selling the first such item to appear on blockchain. It gives away many of its 3D pattern files to its audience of digital creators, encouraging them to create their own iterations of garments. The Fabricant's clothing is available across multiple digital spaces such as social, gaming, and marketplace environments.

B. Make what you sell

"Circular design will drive the decoupling of profit from overproduction in the fashion industry and enable the cultivation of more meaningful customer relationships."

Nicole Bassett
Co-Founder
The Renewal Workshop

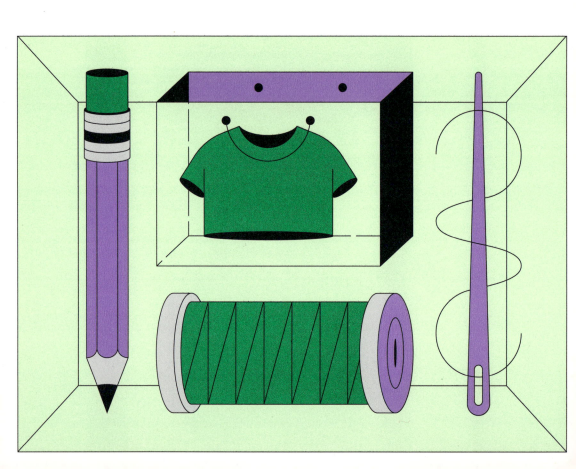

How might we ensure we never end up with deadstock or surplus?

Why?

The fashion industry currently overproduces, resulting in significant amounts of unsold clothing, which lead to extra costs and environmental impacts.

What?

Moving from a design → make → sell model to a design → sell → make model would mean there is no overproduction or unsold stock. This is often referred to as *on-demand manufacturing* or *made to order*.

Who is pioneering it?

- Men's lifestyle company Taylor Stitch started off as a custom shirt maker but quickly moved towards on-demand manufacturing. On Taylor Stitch's own internal crowdfunding platform, customers can pre-order products that have not yet been manufactured. The company then uses the pre-orders as a demand signal to buy the right level of inventory.

- Thanks to artificial intelligence and robotics, manufacturer Teemill has been able to optimise its supply chain, thus reducing its printing and shipping time. Garments are only printed with their final design when they are ordered by a customer, reducing inventory and waste.

- Software company Unmade developed the operating platform UnmadeOS, enabling fashion and sportswear companies to move to a customised, demand-driven production model. UnmadeOS combines automation and visualisation technologies with in-depth integration into the apparel supply chain. The platform enables brands to deliver increased product variety to market and manufacture only what has been bought by customers in real time, thus reducing unsold stock and the proportion of waste.

C. Use safe, recycled, renewable inputs

How might we design products made from safe and recycled or renewable inputs?

"Circular design is also about ensuring there is no *leakage* in the system that would harm nature. For instance, practices that use materials that impoverish soils or pollute oceans cannot be part of a circular design."

Geraldine Vallejo
Sustainability Programme Director
Kering

Why?

The fashion industry currently uses large quantities of materials that, in many cases, are plastic-based and non-renewable. Renewable materials are often grown using methods that are damaging to the environment.

In addition, some of the chemicals used in the dyeing and finishing processes of clothes are known to be harmful to human health.[22]

When washed, clothes can release microfibres that end up contaminating the ocean and freshwater. Those microfibres can be from plastic-based fibres, which do not biodegrade, but can also come from natural fibres whose chemical treatments render them non-biodegradable.[23] Any toxic chemicals used on the fibres can be transported into the waterways.

What?

Making a product from safe inputs means that the health of the people and ecosystems involved in its production and use are protected. Products and materials, and their respective production, are free from hazardous substances and therefore do not release any into the environment. Any microfibres that may cause harm are prevented from reaching the environment, either by changing how clothes are made or by collecting microfibres that are unavoidably shed.

Making a product from recycled inputs means that the need for virgin resources is minimised by using existing fashion products and materials. Where virgin resources are needed, these come from renewable sources grown using regenerative production practices.

Who is pioneering it?

○ Alex de Betak is the creative force behind Bureau Betak — a fashion show, event, and exhibition producer for brands including Dior, Saint Laurent, Fendi, Kenzo, Jacquemus, and many others. Bureau Betak has put in place ten commandments to implement when producing a fashion event, which include eliminating single-use plastics, using renewable energy, and giving a second life to decors whenever possible.

○ Italian mill Candiani Denim has launched a stretch fabric entirely made from renewable sources. In contrast to conventional materials used to achieve elasticity in denim, which come from non-renewable resources, COREVA™ Technology relies on a natural elastomer sourced from rubber trees that is blended with organic cotton. Through the development of this fabric, Candiani has taken a step towards creating stretch denim that will be kept in the system through composting when it can no longer be used.

○ Apparel manufacturer Hirdaramani is moving to eliminate pumice stones and drastically reduce acid washes, which are known to be harmful to workers and the environment. The group uses laser finishes on denim to reduce manual processes, as well as ozone technology and advanced washing technologies to cut its usage of water and chemicals.

ALEX DE BETAK

○ Shanghai-based brand Icicle seeks to bring the symbiotic relationship between human and nature, so deeply rooted in Chinese culture, to the forefront of its approach to fashion. Cashmere, linen, wool, silk, and cotton are Icicle's five core materials and are used in their natural colours (undyed) or dyed with plants.

○ Inditex — the group behind globally recognised brands including Zara, Pull&Bear, Oysho, and Stradivarius — has created the Join Life label, giving users visibility on how its garments are produced and what they are made from. The label highlights which clothing is made with materials such as organic cotton, recycled polyester, and Tencel™ lyocell — all of which typically have a lower environmental impact than other conventional materials — as well as whether production processes run on renewable energy or consume a lot of water. The proportion of Inditex garments that are Join Life rose to 25% in 2020.[24]

○ Kering — the global luxury group and owner of Gucci, Saint Laurent, and Bottega Veneta, amongst other brands — has activated two major levers in order to scale renewable or recycled materials in its collections: the Kering Standards for raw materials and manufacturing processes, which the group made publicly available, and a Materials Innovation Lab based in Italy.[25]

○ Gucci is designing with circular economy principles in mind. Gucci Off The Grid — the first collection under its new Gucci Circular Lines — launched in June 2020 with five product ranges, including accessories, ready-to-wear, and luggage. The collection's main material is ECONYL®, a recycled nylon obtained from pre- and post-customer waste such as abandoned fishing nets and carpets.

○ Teemill, a garment manufacturer based on the Isle of Wight, UK and in India has implemented an effective process to recirculate used water. After dyeing the fabrics, the water flows through a recovery, cleaning, and recirculation process, ensuring 95% of the water used is safe enough for drinking.

○ Vivienne Westwood has put in place a system to source fibres that are organic, regenerative, or recycled and use low-impact dyeing and processing. Organic and recycled cotton, linen, and hemp and fabric innovations such as Ecovero™, Tencel™ lyocell are used more while polyester and acrylic are used less or replaced by recycled or renewable alternatives.

D. Create zero manufacturing waste

How might we make clothes that produce zero waste in the manufacturing process?

"Zero-waste design is not just a method of design, it is a way of thinking. It enforces a holistic way of thinking that deals with systemic, technological, and expressional aspects of garments."

Dr Holly McQuillan
Zero Waste Design Researcher
Critical Textile Topologies

Why?	When making clothes, at least 12% of materials are wasted during the manufacturing or production stage (with some experts estimating the figure to be much higher).[26] This results in significant extra costs and environmental impact due to materials that will never be used.
What?	Eliminating waste at the design, production, and manufacturing stages by, for example, using offcuts from the studio or factory floor in the design of new products or designing product patterns that are zero-waste from the outset. New technologies have proven useful in developing zero-waste techniques. Examples include whole-garment knitting, digital printing of garment shapes, digital 3D sampling, and the application of artificial intelligence technologies to optimise pattern design, resulting in fewer offcuts and waste materials.
Who is pioneering it?	○ Fashion technology company Alvanon has developed 3D design technology that allows designers to create virtual prototypes and test and fit them on a large spectrum of sizes. 3D design helps reduce the waste associated with creating physical prototypes and improve the realistic fit of garments. Since 2001, the company has dedicated itself to body shape data research and gathered in excess of 1.5 million body scans in more than 30 countries, most recently in China, Colombia, Costa Rica, and the US. This has allowed Alvanon to develop thousands of fit standards for hundreds of brands globally.[27]
	○ ASOS's approach to zero-waste design techniques helped the brand spark a new creative outlook on the design process. By rethinking the traditional methods of pattern cutting, collaborating with suppliers and *letting the fabric shape the design*, ASOS has been able to design zero-waste products across multiple product categories.
	○ Hallotex, a design and manufacturing services company, offers fast-fashion companies the opportunity to use the waste they generate in the manufacturing process to create new products.
	○ Redress, an environmental NGO working to reduce waste in the fashion industry and the organiser of the Redress Design Award fashion design competition, offers free online courses and educational materials to designers and educators on circular fashion with a specific focus on textile waste. Redress' zero-waste guide includes several zero-waste techniques, such as draping, knitting, and using a zero-waste pattern.[28]
	○ Shima Seiki, a precision engineering company, developed a knitting technology that can produce entire garments — including the arms, collars, and other parts that would normally be produced separately and then sewn together — on a single machine using a single thread.[29] Shima Seiki also collaborated with UNIQLO to develop 3D knitwear without generating any waste in the process.

②

"Circular design requires thinking backwards and forwards. Thinking back to even before creating the garment and thinking ahead to its many lives."

Carmen Gama
Design and Production Manager
Eileen Fisher
Renew / Waste No More

CIRCULATE PRODUCTS AND MATERIALS

Increasing the number of times products are used is the most direct way to reduce the industry's environmental impact while creating opportunities for better growth. How might we think of *users*, rather than *consumers*?

There are many ways that fashion products and materials can be kept in use and circulated through circular design. A number are already being explored by creatives today.

Each of these strategies can and should be combined to achieve greater results. Also, circulating products and materials to keep them in use does not end with these strategies. The creative possibilities are endless, and these models can be built on in the future.

SHANTANU MEHRA

NIKHIL MEHRA

India's rich heritage and culture is world renowned, and the community is at the centre of everything. The concept of circular economy stems from the belief of being part of each other's lives and sub-consciously shines through with a shared feeling of acceptance.

For instance, in India, there is a deep-rooted tradition of wearing pre-owned clothes, whether they are garments handed down to newborns, family heirlooms or wedding trousseaus passed down through generations of Indian families. It is considered a symbolic representation of our heritage.

For decades now, these traditions have been instrumental in minimising their carbon footprint and, at the same time, forming the very essence of a *spiritual India*.

To us, circular design is all about conserving energy and having an emotional connection with clothing. Hence, we value *hands* more than *heads* as the mind is always in a hurry to do things but the hands only allow you to go at a certain speed. This is a rhythm that inspires us daily as we create ensembles.

We combine solid sartorial techniques with Indian craftsmanship to develop designs that are mostly customised on demand. This way, we not only avoid inventories piling up but also make sure our garments can be kept in use for longer. We make special bespoke ceremonial garments and offer buy-back programmes to our customers so they can return their outfit and we can reinvent it and put it back in good use.

"Circular design is all about conserving energy and having an emotional connection with clothing."

ZHANG NA

"For the fashion industry to be circular in the next ten years, the beauty of fashion and nature should coexist."

I came back to Shanghai in 2004, having studied fashion design at MOD'ART International, a fashion school based in Paris, and started my brand FAKE NATOO in 2008. I noticed that, as trends go by, often what was a must-have a few weeks earlier is then disposed of so quickly and with little thought. I began to wonder, *what's the point of my designs?*

In 2011, after a long reflection, I created a new lifestyle brand, Reclothing Bank, with the idea to reuse, recycle and rebirth clothes. I was challenged by many. Most people thought I wouldn't have enough time to properly set up an initiative like that and that it was too risky. But I insisted. *What's the point of my designs?* The question lingered on in my mind, coming back again and again.

Then something happened, a click. I have a friend who runs a second-hand charity store in Beijing where they hire women to sort, clean, and disinfect old clothes. Those clothes are then shipped to Shanghai. I decided to redesign those old clothes into 30 different coats to be sold in stores around Beijing. They all sold out within a few days. Through recycling, design, handmade patchwork, natural and environmentally-friendly fibres, recycled fabrics, and other methods, we gave a new life to the clothes, improved resource consumption, and reduced pollution.

After years of exploring and a long journey, Reclothing Bank has reached a very high level of circularity. But the journey doesn't end here. For the fashion industry to be circular in the next ten years, the beauty of fashion and nature should coexist.

SAMUEL YANG

ERIK LITZÉN

"Contemporary fashion should also be about education."

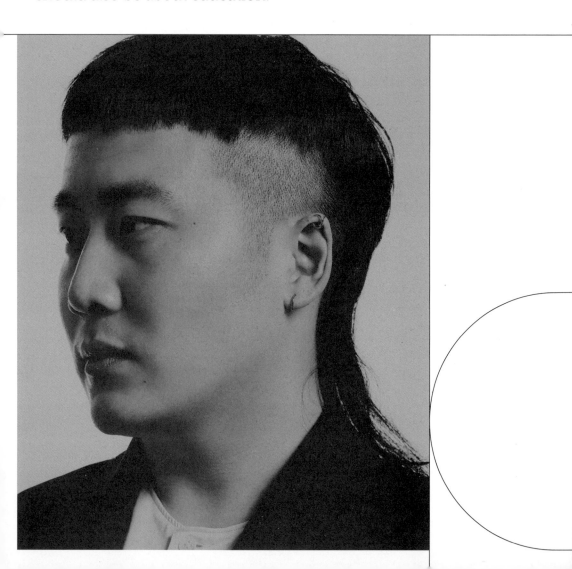

I believe in fashion as something that can be anchored in culture rather than just in consumption and trends, and that's something Erik Litzén, Samuel Yang's co-creative director, Caroline Wåglund, our CEO, and I are passionate about realising through our work.

We want to encourage a deeper connection to belongings in general, a more respectful way of treating them. Fashion today encourages the idea of renewing your look and your identity constantly, but I believe that it's more interesting to slowly cultivate it.

Fashion today is promoted as something so instant that designers also present their ideas with a very short lifespan in mind. We take a different approach, developing long-lasting products based on design decisions that stand the test of time. We don't just move from one design to the next. Instead we always try to reinforce our designs from past seasons to make sure the receiver understands that the ideas we put out two years ago are still viable and lovable.

Contemporary fashion should also be about education. We are not creating new styles every season because the style we created in past seasons is not something we've moved on from. It is a style we are slowly cultivating and fine-tuning over time.

By

Samuel Yang

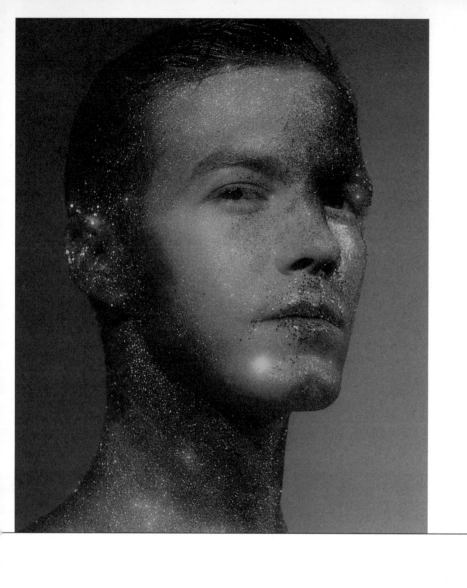

KEVIN GERMANIER

"When you think about sustainable fashion, you think beige, green, linen trousers, etc. And I wanted to show it can be glamorous, shiny, high-end, and desirable."

It all started after I won the Redress Design Award in 2015. I got a work placement in Hong Kong and one day I was asked to go to an industrial area to see leftover fabrics. When I arrived there, I saw an old man digging a hole and throwing beads in it. Those beads were so glamorous and precious and yet they were trashed! I couldn't let that happen. This is when I thought I had to do something to change people's perception of what a sustainable brand should look like. When you think about sustainable fashion, you think beige, green, linen trousers, etc. And I wanted to show it can be glamorous, shiny, high-end, and desirable.

I used to say that at Germanier, we are not producing anything. We are not creating our own buttons, our own prints, our own zippers, or anything really. We do the exact opposite of what students are being taught at school. At school, you are told to first start with a mood board, then come up with a colour palette, and from there go find the fabrics that match the palette. If the fabrics don't match, then your whole story doesn't work. Well, I do the total opposite. I first find my *trash*, which gives me my colour palette, and then I create my mood board.

E. Make fashion that lasts

How might we design clothes that retain their physical integrity?

"Building products that last is the best thing we can do. We believe in designing products that wear in, not out, so they look more beautiful with age."

Michael Maher
Co-Founder and CEO
Taylor Stitch

Why?	Between 2000 and 2015, the global production of clothing doubled, while the average number of times clothes are worn before being thrown away decreased by over a third.[30]
What?	Designing products that are both physically durable and desirable means considering the look, feel, and function of clothing with longevity in mind and informing users on the best way to take care of their clothes.
Who is pioneering it?	

○ Thomas Burberry established Burberry when he was just 21 years old and founded it on the principle that clothing should be designed to be durable, long-lasting, and protect people from the British weather. Thomas's invention of gabardine — the hardwearing and weatherproof fabric — revolutionised rainwear and meant that Burberry's iconic trench coat was designed to last, passed down from generation to generation. This is a principle that Burberry is still guided by today — ensuring everything the brand designs withstands the test of time.

○ Beauty brand La Bouche Rouge redesigns beauty items like lipstick and mascara and tackles the issues generated by disposable beauty products by offering a reusable lipstick bar holder. Made with leather and long-lasting materials, the lipstick holder can be kept by the user over time, and the lipstick bar can be refilled when needed.

○ Lacoste, famous for its classic polo shirt, has implemented a durability protocol to maximise the lifespan of its products. First, data is collected from previous customers (either from quality feedback or targeted surveys) and then an internal testing protocol is developed together with the company's own manufacturing plants. This internal protocol covers individual component testing, as well as finished product testing. The tests are performed on products after washing, and corrective action is taken when failures occur, until a target number of washes is achieved.

○ The fabrics division of W. L. Gore & Associates is pioneering strategies to address the longevity of outerwear garments at the design stage. Through the observation of reclaimed used products and extensive field testing, weaknesses are identified. This enables the brand to set up product-specific lab test schemes to mimic real-use ageing and increase the durability of the components that fail first and think about ways to make the parts more repairable to prolong the useful life of GORE-TEX products.

F. Reconnect people and clothing

"People get deeply attached to stories. Fashion is not so much about producing clothes for me now, it's more related to art and storytelling."

Rudo Nondo
Head of Creative Design
The African Rack

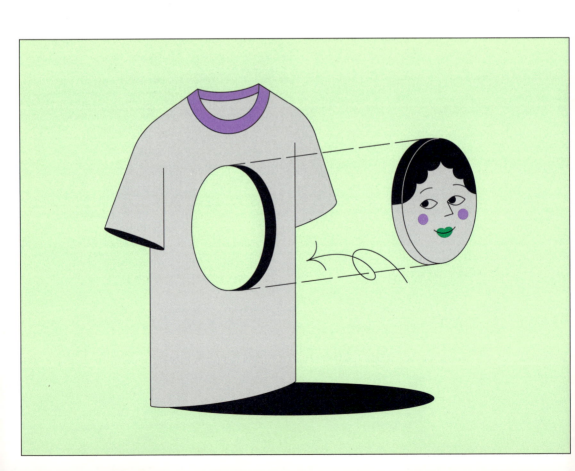

How might we design clothes that users feel emotionally connected to?

Why?

When clothing fits our body, values, and personality, we want to keep it forever.

What?

Using personalisation, craftsmanship, and storytelling to increase the emotional connection between people and their products.

Who is pioneering it?

- Fashion brand and service platform Atelier & Repairs is sourcing clothes that already exist — unsold deadstock from brands and retailers, second quality production, and post-customer unwanted apparel — and transforming them into one-of-a-kind pieces that tell the story of the enduring quality of their original manufacturing. Each piece is redesigned one at a time with the ethos of promoting the artfulness that making new from old can offer. By concentrating on clothing as an expression of individuality and bringing back this tailoring and customisation at the personal and industrial scales, customers can connect to the story of the garment and take pride in knowing it is one of a kind and one less garment made new. Atelier & Repairs' mission is to create a new standard by using the leftovers of today to create the clothing of tomorrow.

- klee klee (meaning *slow down*) is a Shanghai-based brand designing for both emotional and physical durability. Its designs are classic minimalist styles produced using safe natural materials that are bio-based and undyed. Each piece is accompanied by a detailed story so customers can learn where the materials come from, how the garment was made, and how to take care of it, helping to create a stronger bond between the customer and the clothes, ensuring they will be worn longer and more often.

- Rudo Nondo is a fashion designer based in Zimbabwe. After spending two years working with communities in Eswatini, Rudo started sketching based on the stories of the women she met. She produced a collection locally, which she exhibited in several artistic venues and was accompanied by a book and a film telling the story behind the clothes.

G. Take back and repair

"Through repair, customers reconnect emotionally with their items, which incentivises buying better in the future."

Thaís Cipolletta
Co-Founder and Head Of Atelier
The Restory

How might we design businesses and services that enable worn-out or damaged products to be used again?

Why? In the UK, 19% of clothes are discarded because they are damaged, stained, have lost shape or are worn out.[31]

What? Users are empowered to care for and repair their own garments or can bring their garment back to the retailer, brand, or repair service provider for it to be repaired to good-as-new condition.

Who is pioneering it?

- Innovation and quality are the cornerstones of Burberry's approach to design, ensuring its luxury products retain their appeal and value for generations. To support this, Burberry offers its customers a global luxury aftercare service, which includes repairs as well as trench coat reproofing — a special treatment that maintains the signature waterproof characteristics of the Burberry trench coat.

- The Take Care programme by H&M aims to prolong the life of fashion products. Through their repair, remake and refresh initiatives, the garments brought back to their stores can get a new life.

- Fashion brand Phipps International offers a buying and reselling service for vintage items, in addition to its own products. The brand only repairs the pieces that need it and encourages its customers to adopt a customising mindset to prolong the garment's lifecycle, as well as its individuality and the story behind it.

- The Renewal Workshop offers a service to brands and retailers to recover and resell unsellable, returned, or discarded apparel that would otherwise be deemed waste, thus saving inventory from being burned or landfilled.

- Aftercare services offered by The Restory increase the lifetime and desirability of luxury fashion products. The Restory is brand agnostic and provides services to repair, restore and personalise shoes, bags and clothing. Through this service, customers can start seeing the items they own as investments with an emotional and financial value and reconnect with existing items they own that need aftercare.

H. Use data for durability

"By providing brands with information about the wear and failures of their products, they can design better, longer-lasting products and explore more circular business models."

John Atcheson
Co-Founder and CEO
Sellalong

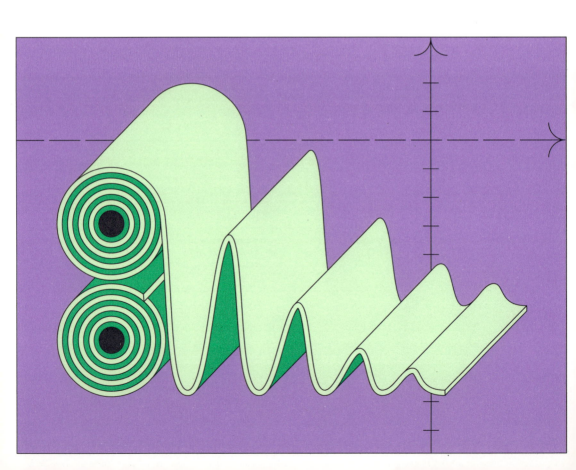

How might we learn from wear-and-tear data to design more durable products?

Why? Designers, brands, and retailers rarely have access to information on what happens to products after they are sold, including how well they withstand wear and tear.

What? Designing processes to capture and gather information on where products fail and using this information to make better design decisions.

Who is pioneering it?

- The Renewal Workshop takes discarded apparel and textiles from a large pool of returned or damaged items, customer take-back programs, and other production sources. It renews them for resale, uses them for upcycled materials, or sends them to be recycled. Upon arrival at the Renewal Workshop premises, each garment is inspected by hand to determine if there are any problems such as holes, broken components, dirt, or stains. This information about where an item breaks or wears out can be used by brands to improve the future design of their garments.

- Sellalong offers an instant buy-back platform for fashion items. When processing each item, Sellalong is able to collect detailed information about each item received (general condition, areas on the items that wear out, how much they resell for, etc.). Sellalong can then provide information back to its customers on how to better care for their items, but also to brands and retailers for them to improve their designs and explore more circular business models.

I. Create an online wardrobe

"Extending the life of your garments just went a step further: you can now extend your entire wardrobe to someone else. As we like to say, what's mine is yours."

Eshita Kabra-Davies
Founder
By Rotation

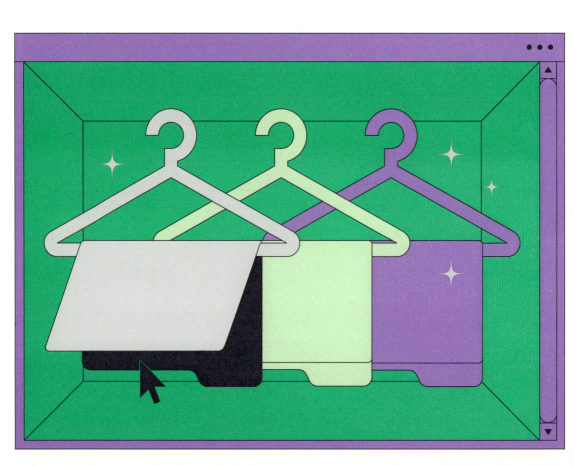

How might we design services so people can access a wide array of products without owning them?

Why?
Whether clothes are owned for everyday life or specific occasions, many are left untouched in our wardrobes.

What?
Users access a large variety of clothes by either paying a one-off fee to use an item for a set period of time or by paying a subscription with a fixed weekly or monthly price. Users can then choose what to wear from physical wardrobes and/or digital catalogues offered by clothing-as-a-service providers.

Who is pioneering it?

○ Peer-to-peer fashion rental business By Rotation provides a mobile application that enables users to hire and rent items on a per-day basis at a fraction of their retail price. By keeping prices low and promoting more socioeconomic and inclusive products, By Rotation also hopes to appeal to more demographics.

○ In 2020, H&M Group released new business models including Singular Society — a subscription service that offers responsibly sourced, high-quality products at the price they cost to make. The Group's Nordic lifestyle brand ARKET is set to begin renting out products from its children's collection through a new partnership with Amsterdam-based online shop and clothing subscription Circos.

○ Clothing rental service YCloset provides access to fashionable clothing by offering both one-off rental and unlimited subscription services. At the time of writing, YCloset had over 10 million returning one-off rental users and one million monthly subscribers and was operating in about 40 cities in China, including Beijing, Shanghai, Guangzhou, and Shenzhen.

J. Pass products
from one user
to the next

"There's more clothing out there than humanity will ever need. Let's circulate products to prolong usage!"

Dounia Wone
Chief Sustainability and Inclusion Officer
Vestiaire Collective

How might we design services so products can seamlessly pass from one user to the next?

Why?   In the UK, 42% of clothes are discarded because they do not fit anymore and 26% because people do not like them anymore.[32]

What?   Brands, retailers, or users swap or resell their garments.

Who is pioneering it?

- thredUP, the online consignment and thrift store, has grown into one of the world's largest resale platforms for women's and kids' apparel, shoes and accessories, transforming resale with technology and a mission to inspire people to purchase second-hand first. To achieve this, one of the biggest hurdles thredUp had to overcome was breaking down the stigma of second-hand and making buying used clothing online just as easy and fun as shopping new. As the business grew, thredUP scaled the way the items were listed and, through technologies, is now able to process 100,000 pre-loved items every day. To date, thredUP has processed over 100 million unique second-hand items from 35,000 brands across 100 categories.

- Resale platform Vestiaire Collective facilitates the selling and buying of pre-owned pieces through its digital platform. It extends the lifespan of pieces people no longer wear by bringing them back into circulation and encourages them to care about their items and maximise their resale value. Through Vestiaire Collective's collaboration with Alexander McQueen, loyal customers of McQueen are invited to return the items they no longer use in exchange for credit to spend in store, and Vestiaire Collective offers these formerly owned pieces from the fashion house on a dedicated page on their app.

K. Remake and restyle

"The idea behind restyling pieces
is to celebrate the circular economy,
elevating historical artifacts
in the garments we choose to sell."

Spencer Phipps
Founder
Phipps International

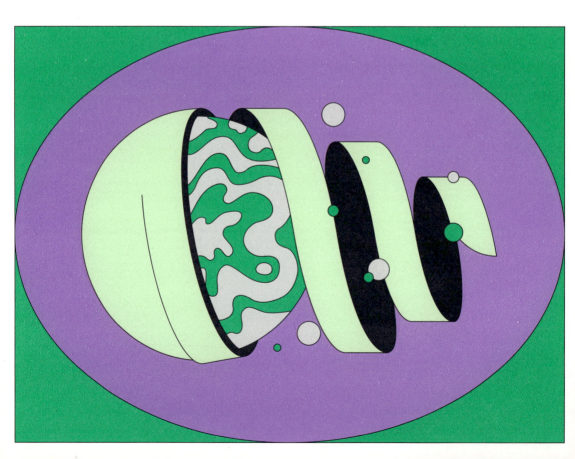

How might we revamp or remake old fashion products into new ones?

Why? Currently, 87% of clothing is landfilled or incinerated after its final use.[33]

What? Remaking and restyling fashion items to extend the life of the piece or the materials it is made from.

Who is pioneering it?

○ Wholesaler of used goods Bank & Vogue hand-picks used items from around the world for its Beyond Retro retail stores in Europe and its online platform, finding new homes for these products and diverting them from landfill. Beyond Retro has also become a label, reworking carefully selected vintage fabrics into unique fashion pieces available at Beyond Retro stores.

○ Christopher Raeburn's label, RÆBURN, repurposes military and original surplus materials and apparel. These resources are often sourced locally and reimagined into unique garments, objects, and accessories.

○ Fashion retailer Browns commissioned a collection from designer Duran Lantink, asking him to use Browns' stocks from past seasons to create 45 entirely new pieces to be sold in Browns' store.

○ H&M provides a customisation service to ensure garments are kept in use for longer. The service offers embroidery personalisation from prices starting at GBP 3 (about USD 4).[34] The fashion retailer has also published tips on how to customise existing pieces, for example by making a maxi dress into a shorter garment.[35]

L. Use what you have

"Repurposing is the only way forward. There is so much stuff lying around across the world. Beautiful stuff. The challenge is making it even more beautiful than it already was."

Duran Lantink
Designer

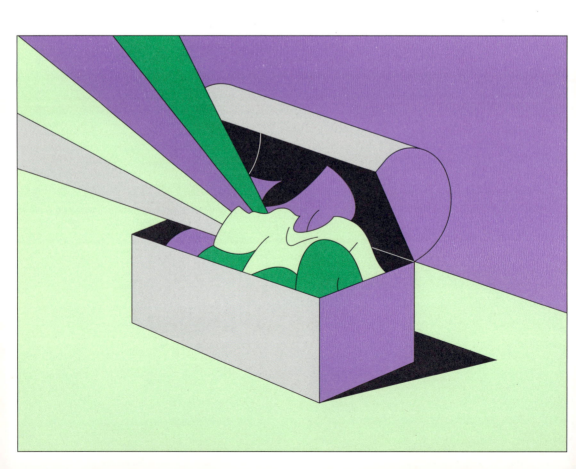

How might we design clothes using what we already have rather than making or producing them from scratch?

Why?

The equivalent of one truckload full of textiles goes to landfill or is incinerated every second.[36] These materials could be used to make new items.

What?

Instead of sourcing materials specially produced for a specific design, materials are sourced from what is already available on the market, including existing clothes and material offcuts.

Who is pioneering it?

O   Gabriela Hearst bases her design process on the use of high-quality deadstock fabric. This process pushed her to rethink her design process. By sourcing the fabric first, Gabriela and her team have to work backwards, first quantifying the number of pieces they can make. While this design process can seem more complicated on the surface, the team at Gabriela Hearst has found that it provides structure and enables efficient production and shipping.

O   Jaypore is an Indian artisanal brand from Aditya Birla Fashion and Retail Limited that preserves the country's heritage and stories. By reusing sarees handed down from generations, the brand increases the life of the materials by creating contemporary and longer-lasting pieces.

O   MARINE SERRE uses towels, silk scarves, denim, pillowcases, bedsheets, jewels, leather, and other used materials to create her garments. A full-time employee at the brand is responsible for sourcing these materials from France and surrounding countries.[37] The materials are then cleaned and taken apart to be used in new designs created within the constraints of the materials.

M. Make to be made again

How might we design clothes so they are made to be made again — able to be disassembled and their components reused, remade or their materials recycled?

"Apparel designed for the circular economy are those that can be repaired, reused and remade infinitely."

Nicole Bassett
Co-Founder
The Renewal Workshop

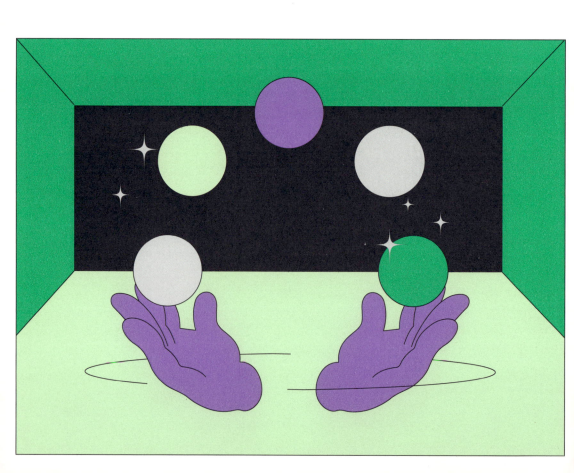

Why?

Today less than 1% of clothes[38] are recycled into new clothes. This is due to clothing being created without considering its ability to be recycled, for example by using complex material blends or hard to separate components. This limits the incentives to invest in collection and recycling infrastructure, making high levels of recycling even more difficult to achieve.

What?

Designing clothes so that when they can no longer be used, their materials and constituent parts — including threads, trims and fillings — can be turned into new parts, fabric, and clothes.

Designing clothes that are easy to disassemble because their buttons, zips, and embellishments are quick to remove or that are made from only one material. These two strategies keep materials in use by facilitating recyclability.

To make sure recycling can then take place in practice, these material and product design choices must go hand in hand with the deployment of effective collection and recycling infrastructure.

Who is pioneering it?

○ adidas has created FUTURECRAFT.LOOP — shoes made from a single material, making them easily recyclable. Achieving this required several material and manufacturing innovations. On the materials front, designers worked to ensure all the components of the shoe, from the laces to the sole, could be made from the same material. On the manufacturing front, adidas had to find a way to assemble the shoe without using glue, which would have contaminated the recycled material stream. As adidas set out to create a shoe that did not compromise on style or performance, some of the innovations took several years, but the result is a shoe that is designed to generate pure, high-quality recyclate, which can then be made into the next generation of footwear.

○ Napapijri designed its Circular Series jacket — part of its broader Circular Series collection — using a mono-material design: a nylon composition. The jacket is made out of recycled materials and is recyclable at the end of use. Fillings and trims are made of nylon 6, while the fabric is made of ECONYL®, a high-performance nylon 6 yarn recycled from discarded fishing nets and other materials. The fact that the jacket is made from only one material enables it to be turned back into nylon 6 yarn, ready to be used for the next product. When purchasing the jacket, customers can also register it in the Circular Series programme and return it to Napapijri when worn out. Read more about how the Circular Series jacket was designed in page 58.

○ Teemill, a UK-based manufacturer, has eliminated plastic blends from fashion items and put in place a take-back programme. Customers are able to send back their worn-out items to Teemill's warehouse, where an on-site manufacturing facility can then transform them into threads that are used to produce new clothes.

N. Make information available

"Better choices can be made with better information."

Ella Peinovich-Griffith
Founder and CEO
Powered By People

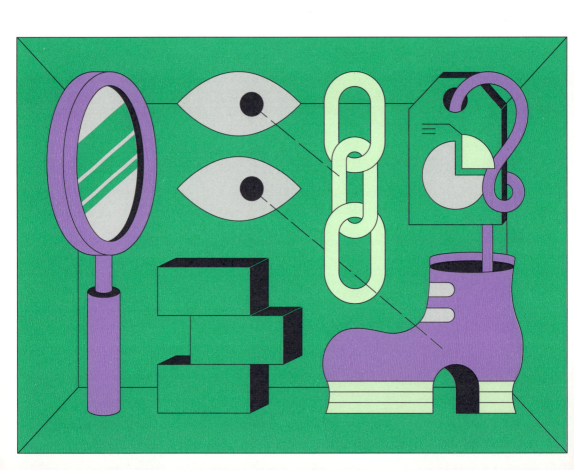

How might we use technology to enable traceability and transparency of products and materials so they can be made in a safe and fair way and kept in use for longer?

Why? Fashion supply chains are global and complex, and the materials will likely pass through many factories and countries before ultimately being shipped as complete products to stores. This can make it difficult for users, brands, and retailers to fully trace where the products and materials they use come from, what they are made of, and who they are made by.

Even when the supply chain can be traced back to the source, there is often little information shared about each stage of the process, for example the working conditions of factory employees or the safety data on dyes or finishing treatments.

This lack of transparency and traceability can make it difficult to guarantee the elimination of poor and unsafe working conditions or the negative environmental impacts of supply chains.

What? Using technologies and activities to enable greater transparency and traceability. Technologies such as RFID, blockchain, and DNA tagging can be used to trace product specifications, chemical inputs, materials used, and production practices.

Designing the information systems and providing transparency to support reuse and after-use practices such as sorting, remaking, and recycling. This also enables fairer and safer working conditions to be established along the supply chain by making it clear what and where there are issues to be overcome.

Who is pioneering it?

○ EON is a platform for bringing physical products online to connect fashion, apparel, and retail end-to-end. EON's platform, Network & CircularID™ Protocol, enables brands to create a digital identity for each item. This digitisation supports brands in scaling circular business models as they are able to manage the lifecycle of their products and materials from production through use, recommerce, recycling and regeneration. This helps customers access information about their product and enables brands to better understand customer behaviours, increase product use, and identify materials for disassembly and recycling.[39]

○ Fashion Revolution, a not-for-profit global movement created in 2013 by Carry Somers and Orsola de Castro, publishes its annual *Transparency Index* report, ranking 250 of the world largest fashion brands and retailers according to how much they disclose about their social and environmental policies, practices, and impacts.

○ Provenance is a leading software platform for supply chain and impact transparency. Enabled by blockchain, mobile, and open data, the technology supports brands that want to share verified information on the origin, journey, and impact of their products with users and stakeholders.[40] In collaboration with Martine Jarlgaard, Provenance tracked the world's first garment with a unique ID that held location mapping, content, and timestamps from every step of production, making this journey accessible via the garment's smart label.[41] Provenance also worked with Haikure, an Italian brand, to map the journey of their jeans, from the provenance of their buttons, lining, and fabric to the processes and actors involved in making the jeans, from sourcing to market.

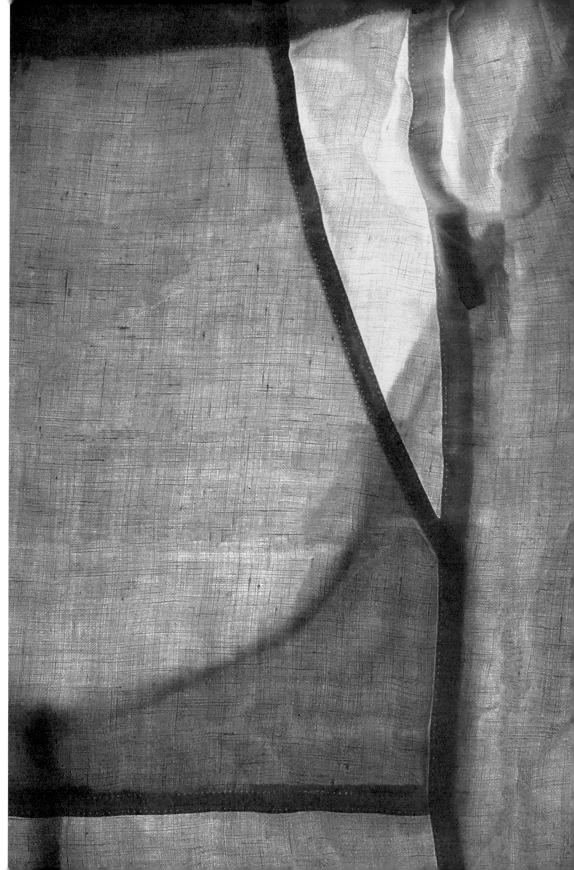

(3)

"The fashion industry has an extensive agricultural footprint, so by reforming it, you have a monumental space to create a positive impact."

Linus Mueller
R&D Lead
Circular Systems

Currently, materials in the fashion industry come from two sources. About 60% come from finite resources such as oil and other fossil fuels[42] — these are used to make plastic-based fibres including polyester, nylon, acrylic, and elastane. The remainder comes from renewable resources — these include cellulose-based fibres (for example cotton, hemp, flaxseed, viscose, and lyocell) and protein-based fibres (for example wool and silk). Due to conventional farming methods that use large amounts of synthetic fertilisers and pesticides, renewable and finite resource use are often intrinsically linked.

Over time, fashion production should be decoupled from the consumption of finite resources.

In the first instance, this means using already existing materials to make new clothes and remaking and recycling to keep the materials in use.

Where new materials are still needed, they should, over time, only come from renewable resources grown using regenerative production practices. Regenerative production practices can build soil health, help tackle climate change by sequestering carbon, increase water quality and biodiversity, and improve the resilience of ecosystems.

The regenerative mindset focuses on achieving positive outcomes rather than merely doing less harm.[43]

There are many ways for the fashion industry to actively regenerate nature.

This chapter presents examples of creatives who are already adopting regenerative practices.

These are only some examples. The creative possibilities to ensure natural systems are regenerated are endless, and these models can be built on in the future.

RUDO NONDO

"My quest for materials is no longer in the conventional fabric store."

After living in the UK for a few years, I came back to Zimbabwe in 2009. I started working in the fashion space in 2013. As I was sourcing garments and materials locally, I noticed a change in our design industry as a result of an economic collapse that initiated a rapid decline in factories manufacturing clothes and a handful of local designers working in the clothing and accessories space. I noted with great concern that Western countries were sending more of their used clothes to our country, and with a rapid decline in our economy, many people had started moving away from shopping in traditional clothing stores and were starting to source clothes that were coming in the bales. We still have a lot of clothing bales coming into our country illegally. Circularity here means focusing on repurposing the textile waste that is shipped to Zimbabwe, diverting it from landfill and prolonging the clothing lifecycle.

As the years have progressed, I have continued with this model, working with women in rural and peri-urban communities. It is here that my journey has taken a turn to storytelling through design. This has led me to use mostly locally sourced material and design with what would be ordinarily termed waste.

Through this process I have started using materials I already have, redesigning old clothes and turning them into new ones, taking old collections apart and reusing the material for new collections. My quest for materials is no longer in the conventional fabric store.

What is even more important to me, beyond producing clothes, are the stories I get to tell via my designs. I don't design for volume, I design to tell stories. One of my collections, *Layers*, was accompanied by a book and a short fashion film that told the stories of women in fashion design and artisans from rural artisan communities in Zimbabwe and Eswatini where I spent 10 months from 2017 to 2018.

It is through this process that I have begun to understand the true meaning of design. Rural artisans view their products as works of art, with meaningful stories behind the designs, colours, and shapes they chose to weave. They use natural dyes from plants, berries, and bark and only work with natural materials that contributed to the growth of the local ecosystem and environment. They are also willing to teach their craft and view it as something that can be passed through generations, preserving the history of their tradition and culture. The system they are part of and contribute to, from the start, is intended for regeneration and restoration. This is the essence of what circular design means to me.

STELLA McCARTNEY

"The circular economy offers exciting business opportunities whilst having a positive effect on the planet. The fashion industry needs to embrace it!"

It still seems crazy to me that less than 1% of material used to produce clothing is recycled into new clothing, meaning 99% of all textiles and fashion are landfilled or incinerated. It's so incredibly wasteful! Facts like these really emphasise why we need to come together as an industry to act now and transform fashion.

As a brand, we are committed to operating in a way that reduces pressure on natural ecosystems, keeps resources in the ground, and allows Mother Nature to heal. When I launched Stella McCartney back in 2001, I committed to never using leather, feathers, skin, or fur in any of our designs. It was completely unheard of back then and still is to this day for a luxury brand. Since then, we've strived to keep pushing the envelope on what sustainable fashion looks like.

We have invested time and creativity into material and supply chain innovation because those are areas where meaningful impacts can be immediately made. We are working on farm-level traceability for our cotton to gain better insight into how it's being grown and soil health. Soil is an important carbon sink so improving soil health is a vital natural climate solution, and we want to make sure we are doing everything we can to mitigate climate change.

The circular economy offers exciting business opportunities whilst having a positive effect on the planet. The fashion industry needs to embrace it!

O. Regenerative as well as renewable

How might we use renewable fibres from sources that regenerate nature rather than deplete it?

Why?

Conventional farming practices used to grow renewable resources such as cotton or wool degrade the soil they rely on, reduce biodiversity, and contribute to pollution and climate change. For example, cotton, which accounts for about 2.5% of the world's cropland, is responsible for 16% of all pesticides used.[43]

What?

Sourcing plant-based fibres — such as cotton, hemp, linen, and wood — to create fibres such as viscose from regenerative agricultural practices or non-edible agricultural by products.

Regenerative production practices aim to improve the health and resilience of the whole ecosystem.[44] Their adoption supports increased biodiversity, including growing a diverse range of fibres that are appropriate for the local conditions while minimising the need for pesticide and fertiliser use.

These practices — such as agroforestry, permaculture, and managed grazing — employ a broad range of agricultural methods depending on local conditions. These methods include using organic composts that build soil carbon and improve soil health and structure, planting rows of trees to act as windbreaks at the edges of fields to shelter crops and prevent soil erosion, avoiding the use of synthetic pesticides and fertilisers, growing different types of crops on a plot of land in different seasons (crop rotation), and growing two or more crops in the same space at the same time (intercropping) including planting food crops between rows of cotton and planting seeds without digging up the ground (employing a no-till or low-till approach).

Materials derived from animals, such as wool and leather, are sourced from producers that integrate livestock into regenerative production systems by using practices such as managed grazing that enables grass to recover and regrow. The grass pulls carbon out of the atmosphere and stores it in the ground, improving soil structure and biodiversity. These practices also make the land more productive in the long term and increase resilience to drought and heavy rain.

Who is pioneering it?

○ Circular Systems uses its Agraloop Bio-Refinery to transform food crop waste (from bananas, pineapples, oilseed flax, etc.) into natural fibre products. Many crops are simply wasted: every year, 270 million tonnes of banana crops are left to rot and 32 million acres of rice straw are burned in India.[46] By buying food crop waste and using it to create natural fibres, Circular Systems provides farmers with extra revenue (from selling the food crop waste) and natural fertiliser generated during the transformation process of the crop into Agraloop BioFibre.

○ FarFarm uses agroforestry to grow fibres in a way that regenerates the soil and provides community development in Brazil. Its main focus is organic cotton, which can produce good quality fibre for the fashion industry and food crops such as corn, rice, beans, and a variety of fruits, which can provide food security for the vulnerable communities FarFarm works with. FarFarm is also testing a spinning process with bananas, jute, pineapple, tucum, and other locally grown natural fibres.

○ Fibershed is a California based non-profit organisation. It started in 2010 when its founder, Rebecca Burgess, committed to developing a prototype wardrobe by working with local talent and sourcing regeneratively grown fibres from within a 150-mile radius of the project's headquarters. Within months, the project became a movement, and the concept of Fibershed spread to various regions across the globe.

○ Kering, Eileen Fisher and Timberland have become Frontier Founders under the Savory Institute's Land to Market programme to promote and support the regenerative production of leather and wool. The three companies use Savory's Ecological Outcome Verification™ (EOV™) in their leather and fibre supply chains.[47] EOV™ is a soil and landscape assessment methodology that tracks outcomes in biodiversity, soil health, and ecosystem function (water cycle, mineral cycle, energy flow, and community dynamics). Farms and ranches demonstrating positively trending outcomes in land regeneration through EOV™ are entered into a Verified Regenerative Supplier Roster from which participating buyers, brands, retailers, and end customers can access products and services that have been produced on a verified regenerative land base.[48]

○ Gucci is working on feasibility studies under its *Natural Climate Solutions Portfolio* with Conservation International, South Pole, and Native to identify and scale up regenerative agriculture projects within its sourcing regions. The aim is to source regenerative raw materials for its products.

REGENERATIVE FARMING

- BIOLOGICALLY ACTIVE SOILS
- LOW INPUT COSTS
- HIGH WATER INFILTRATION AND STORAGE
- HIGH CROP DIVERSITY
- HEALTHY LOCAL ECOSYSTEM
- HIGH WATER HOLDING AND FILTRATION CAPACITY
- LOW HEALTH RISKS TO FARM WORKERS
- TASTY CROPS WITH HIGH MICRONUTRIENT CONTENT
- INCREASED RESILIENCE
- SUPPORT FOR LONG-TERM YIELDS
- MULTIPLE REVENUE STREAMS

"A regenerative circle corresponds to the rhythm of nature; it forms a supportive relationship with ecological systems and future economic growth."

Shaway Yeh
Founder
Yehyehyeh

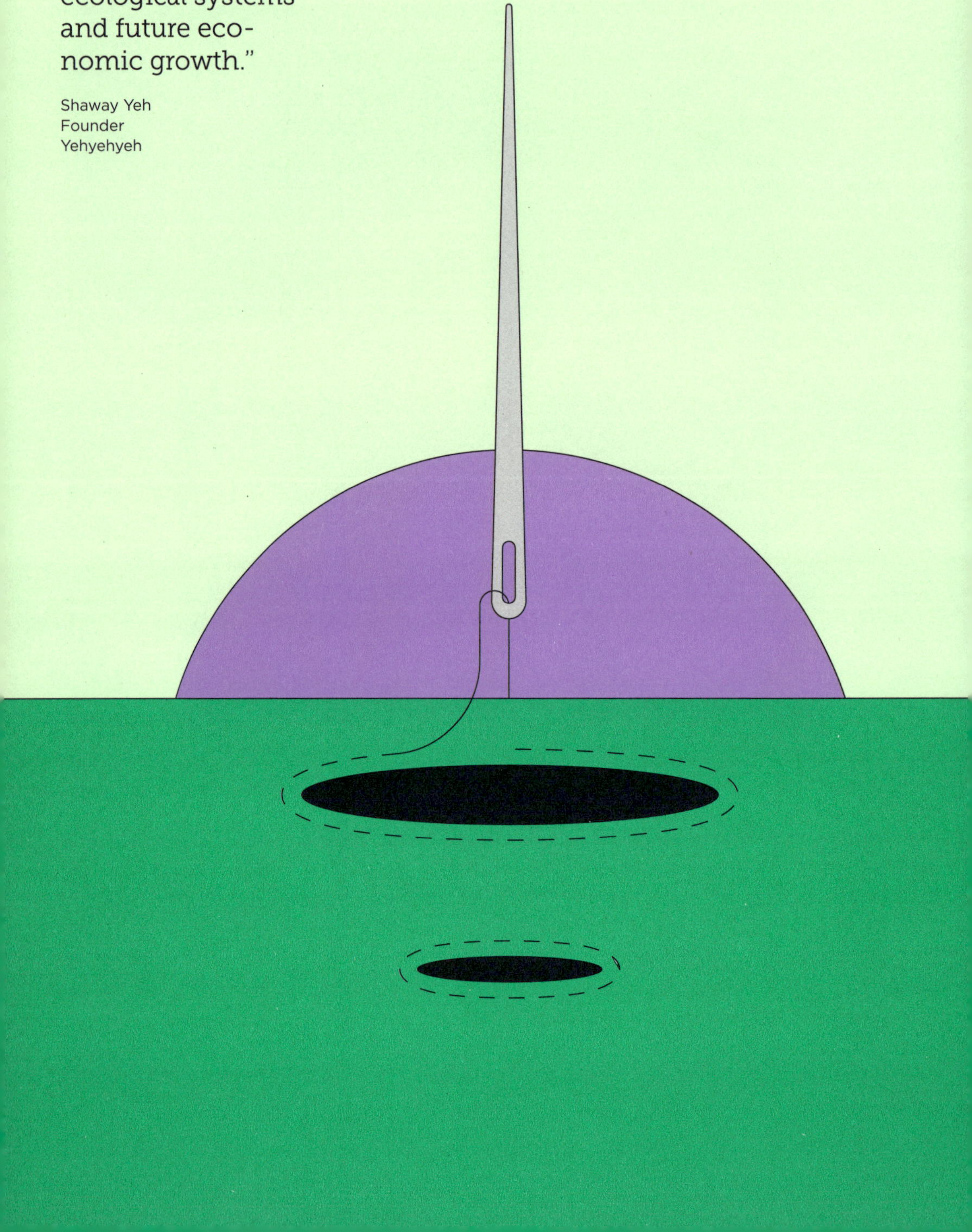

5

HOW TO GET STARTED

"In a circular design approach, design is no longer a step in the value chain but an activity that takes place throughout the whole process."

Sergi Masip Sanz
Circular Economy Project Manager
Hallotex

HOW TO
GET STARTED

Applying systems thinking alongside the three principles of a circular economy reveals a wealth of creative possibilities.

BETHANY WILLIAMS

"I have always been interested in making discarded materials beautiful again."

I have always been interested in making discarded materials beautiful again. Starting out in the industry, I knew I wanted to set up my own practice and create a positive social impact through my activity.

My brand follows this ethos. We only work with recycled, deadstock or organic materials. We work with various garment sorting and recycling facilities both in London and across England. Our knitwear is made in the UK and in Italy by a social cooperative called Manusa that specialises in hand and machine knitting, crochet, and embroidery, and we work with a screen printer from London. Our buttons are also made in London by an experienced craftsperson using Hackney-grown wood harvested by local tree surgeons. Our weaving comes from San Patrignano, an initiative in Italy that uses craft to help marginalised people. They get deadstock yarns from mills and create new materials with them each season.

For each collection, we also work with a specific NGO. For our last collection we collaborated with the Magpie Project, a charity that supports women and children under five in temporary or unsuitable accomodation and those without it. We created a capsule collection of blanket coats made from antique wool blankets that we source from car boot sales and antique shops across the UK. We gave each blanket a new life and shared our profits with Magpie.

I see my work as research first. I feel we are running a research project, and with each one we can achieve more than just fashionable clothing.

MARINE SERRE

"Our conscious approach has evolved around rethinking production chains, making progress on climate neutrality, circularity and product resilience, and reconsidering the way we live."

When I started MARINE SERRE, I asked myself what would keep us here for a long time.

Since its beginnings in 2017, MARINE SERRE has aimed to shake up the industry with a revolutionary ecological shift. Our conscious approach has evolved around rethinking chains of production, making progress on climate neutrality, circularity, resilience of our products, and reconsidering the way we live.

For us, circularity is the ability to create regenerative processes. Climate neutrality has placed a focus on reducing travel and producing locally. Resilience is a call to be humble and a reminder not to exploit the resources that the earth has to offer us. We need to consider the environment in its broadest possible definition and wisely react.

Upcycled and recycled materials are at the centre of our design process. Today, around 50% of our collections are composed of upcycled products. The other half sees us working with innovative and sustainable fibres, such as biodegradable yarns and recycled fibres. As an independent brand, we try to be part of shaping our common future toward a greater consciousness of the body, hybridity, and heterogeneity all taken together within a regenerative consciousness.

It is about rethinking our future. It includes creating a new system and, within it, new supply chains and new ways to consume, share, communicate, work, imagine and experience. It is about a way to live, a way to act and a way to get inspired.

Being conscious is about understanding that humankind is not at the centre of the world, that we are part of a bigger picture. When you start to see things from this perspective, you start to care more about others, the environment, and nature that surrounds us and to which we belong. Consequently, you care more about what you buy, what you eat, what you wear. We want things to make sense in our future world.

Change can only happen if there are many of us on the same path.

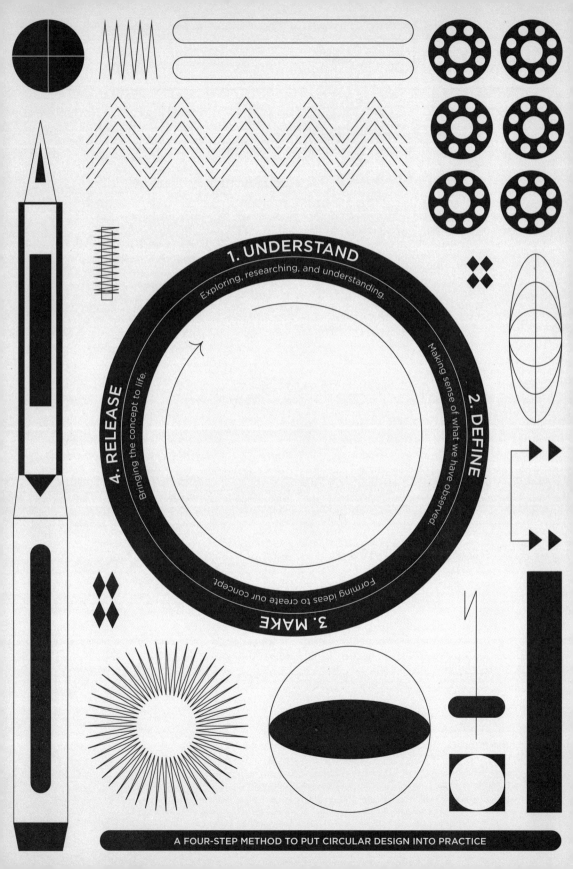

A FOUR-PHASE CIRCULAR DESIGN PROCESS

Now that we know what circular design means for fashion, many ways of incorporating it into existing practices may spring to mind. Yet getting started can still feel like a daunting task. This chapter will help you.

BEFORE WE START, LET'S PICK A CHALLENGE TO TACKLE.

Given the size and complexity of the fashion industry, there are many possible challenges to address. The one you choose will depend on your context, skill sets, values, and capabilities.

EXAMPLE: HOW MIGHT WE ENSURE CLOTHES ARE WORN MORE?

Depending on our role, some of the questions we ask ourselves could be:

- How might we design services that will enable clothes to be worn more?
- How might we create a brand narrative that will generate an emotional bond between our products and our customers?
- How might we tell stories that encourage customers to get more wear out of their clothes?
- How might we design garments that are physically and emotionally durable?

ONCE THE CHALLENGE IS CLEAR, WE PROCEED THROUGH THE CREATIVE PROCESS, EMPHASISING SYSTEMS THINKING THROUGHOUT.

Methodologies such as design thinking can help structure this process, making it easier to get started, accept unknowns, and navigate complexity.

1. UNDERSTAND

This phase is about exploring, researching, and understanding the details of the issues at stake. Different types of research are needed:

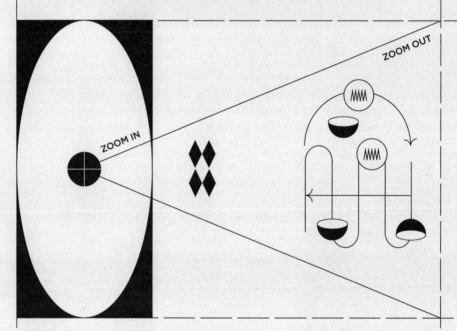

USER RESEARCH

UNDERSTAND WHO WE ARE DESIGNING FOR

In the context of our challenge, this means understanding why and how people currently acquire, use, and dispose of their clothes. These observations will inform the design solution.

STAKEHOLDER RESEARCH

UNDERSTAND WHO WE ARE DESIGNING WITH

This means understanding which people and organisations can help us shape and implement a solution and/or be impacted by it. It means understanding who our key internal and external stakeholders are, how they can contribute to solving the challenge, and what constraints we face.

SYSTEM RESEARCH

UNDERSTAND THE CONTEXTS OF OUR USERS AND STAKE-HOLDERS AND THE RELATIONSHIPS BETWEEN THEM

This means considering the social, economic, technological, and environmental dimensions of your challenge. Understanding relationships in the system and discovering its negative and positive feedback loops help us appreciate its intricacies and ultimately spot new opportunities.

2. DEFINE

This phase is about making sense of what we observed.

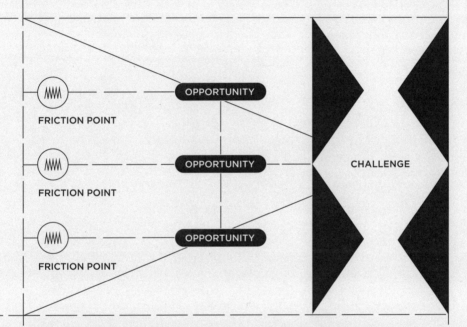

ONCE WE ARE CONFIDENT AND COMFORTABLE WITH OUR RESEARCH, WE CAN ENTER THE <u>DEFINE</u> PHASE IN WHICH WE WILL MAKE SENSE OF WHAT WE OBSERVED BY ASKING OURSELVES:

In the <u>Understand</u> and <u>Define</u> phases we concentrate on solving the right problem, so that in the <u>Make</u> and <u>Release</u> phases, we can focus on solving the problem correctly.

o What are the main friction points?

o Where and what are the design opportunities to tackle those friction points?

o How can we link those insights back to our challenge and the three principles of the circular economy?

3. MAKE

This phase is about forming ideas to create our concept.

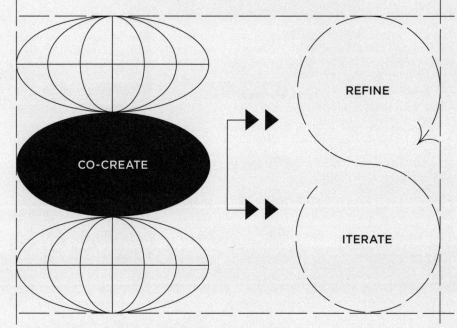

We will need to bring on board all the necessary stakeholders to form ideas and co-create. The more diverse this core team is, the richer the perspectives and solution will be. Including voices from the manufacturing, use, and after-use phases will help us spot moments when waste, pollution, and lost value occur.

We will then refine and iterate our ideas as much as possible. Starting out with a lot of ideas is beneficial. Prioritising and testing ideas early is mandatory. This way we will move from creating tons of ideas to building a concrete concept.

We will need to constantly check that the ideas that are selected are considered with the three principles of the circular economy in mind.

Finally, the time will come for us to test our concept. A concept is never a perfect solution. It will have to be sent out and tested in order to be improved and evolve. Try to test it with a range of users that may interact with our product or service over time. In this way, we can better predict how our concept may impact the wider system.

4. RELEASE

This phase is about bringing the concept to life by piloting it in a chosen context.

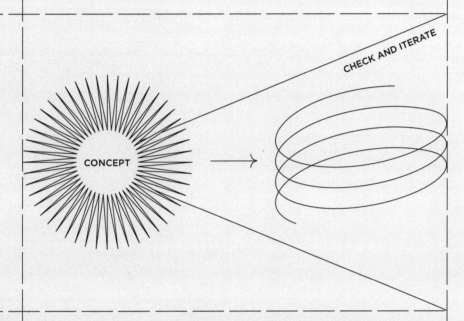

Constantly check how the systems that surround the challenge are evolving and how the stakeholders, actors, and relationships between them are impacted or impact the solution. Iterate the solution accordingly.

The following systems thinking methods can be helpful when undertaking this research.

Employ root cause thinking

It can be tempting to reach directly for the most obvious and immediate solution to a problem. Employing root cause thinking can get to the origin of a problem and uncover a more effective solution.

THE ROOT CAUSE THINKING THAT SAVED MONUMENTS

In the 1990s, monuments in Washington, D.C. were found to be deteriorating at an alarming rate, to the puzzlement of those trying to protect them. While the problem was clear, the solution seemed out of reach. However, employing the *five whys*[49] technique, entomologist Don Messersmith was able to get to the underlying cause of the problem and ultimately propose a solution. He asked the following questions:

o	Why are they deteriorating? Because harsh chemicals are used to clean them.
o	Why are the chemicals needed? To clean the bird droppings.
o	Why are there so many bird droppings? Because the birds eat the spiders around the monuments.
o	Why are there so many spiders near the monuments? Because the insects the spiders eat are drawn there at dusk.
o	Why are the insects drawn there at dusk? Because the way the monuments are lit in the evening attracts them.
Solution	Change the monuments' lighting.

When applying root cause thinking in fashion, consider which *why* questions we need to ask if we come across, for example, customer reluctance to engage in rental or sharing models. What might be the practical, economic, or cultural issues beneath the surface of such reluctance? To what extent can they be addressed by the designer, and which other interventions might be needed?

Understand our sphere of influence

Understanding the extent of our influence requires looking at the impact of the decisions we make on all parts of the system. We might not touch every part of the system directly, but if we have a limited understanding of the system, we might miss a crucial aspect that influences whether our design has a positive or negative impact overall. By understanding our sphere of influence on a system, we can avoid unintended consequences.

GOOD INTENTIONS WITH UNINTENDED CONSEQUENCES

In an effort to reduce the amount of materials they use, many plastic packaging companies have sought to lightweight their packaging over the past 40 years, making it slimmer or smaller. This has led to significant material and cost savings through remarkable innovation in materials science and engineering. Today, a one-litre washing-up liquid bottle uses 64% less material than in the 1970s.[50]

However, lightweighting only takes into account the amount of materials used and whether the packaging still works well. It doesn't consider the impact on other parts of the plastic system. Using systems thinking reveals that the lightweighting trend can have undesirable consequences. While lightweight packaging may be more efficient in production and use, it also means that each piece of packaging has less value after use, particularly given the complex material combinations often applied to achieve lightweighting. If the after-use value of the packaging is too low, there is less incentive to collect and recycle it. As a result, more ends up in landfill or the environment.

When setting out to understand our sphere of influence in the fashion system, it pays to think broadly. A switch to bio-based fabrics like wool and cotton, for example, will have implications for farmers, the broader agricultural system, and, in the end, global land use. Can these implications be positive, and if so how?

Take feedback loops into account

A system is about connectedness and dynamism. It is made of countless diverse relationships that are constantly evolving. Those relationships are the connectors between the different elements that the system is made of. If we design to answer user needs only, we are influencing one element of the system without seeing the bigger picture. Understanding how all the elements of the system interact with each other helps inform design and avoid unintended consequences.

THE FASHION DISCOUNTING LOOP

Each fashion brand or retailer is at liberty to decide whether to discount products, by how much, when, and for how long. If a brand is considering only the impact on their business at a particular moment in time, discounting can be a useful strategy to sell off old stock or drive customers to their sites or into stores. However, when another brand, or many other brands, also decide to discount, or if discounting happens perpetually, prices are driven down across the whole sector. In the end, each brand is making only slim margins on its sale garments, and this also has an impact on the price of fashion overall. It devalues what the industry provides, with ramifications for all those involved in creating garments. This is an example of a negative reinforcing feedback loop, which compounds change in one direction. The change in this case is the constantly dropping retail price of clothing.

However, feedback loops are not always negative. Reinforcing loops can be positive as well. For example, designing clothes that can be remade and recycled could spur an innovation loop that incentivises the development of recycling infrastructure and collection points, which will in turn prompt more designers to create clothes that fit in this system.

Questions to keep in mind on the three principles

These questions can help us keep the three circular economy principles in mind at all times. They will enable us to achieve our goals and ensure our design solutions are doing more good rather than less bad.

ELIMINATE WASTE AND POLLUTION

- How can I use digital technology to reduce the need for physical products while improving the experience and engagement of my customers?
- What production processes can I use to avoid deadstock or inventory? How can I implement demand-driven production processes?
- How can I make sure no hazardous chemicals are used in my processes?
- How can I ensure my product will not release microfibres that may cause harm?
- What processes can ensure energy, water, and chemicals are used effectively to make my product?
- How can I use all the materials and fabrics I buy?

CIRCULATE PRODUCTS AND MATERIALS

- What are the business models that can increase the number of times my product will be used?
- How can I answer the new or evolving needs of my customers without them having to buy new products?
- How can I make sure my product remains desirable and functional for its user or users over time?
- How can I use my product, service, and storytelling to provide clear instructions, helping people take better care of their product?
- How can I gather information about my products — for example, their common failures, how they are used, and why customers stop using them — to improve my design in the future?
- How can I make my product easy to repair?
- How can my product be created from existing clothes or fabrics?
- How can I make my product easy to disassemble so its components and materials can be reused?
- How can I make my product so that its materials can ultimately be recycled?
- What technologies are available to recycle my product and reuse its components?
- How can I inform my customers about what to do with the product once they do not want it anymore? Are those solutions available in practice?
- How can I provide full transparency and traceability about my product to my customers and others in the system?

REGENERATE NATURE

- What regeneratively grown materials can I use in my products?
- How can I support farmers and producers transitioning from conventional to regenerative agricultural practices?
- How can I use materials that are native to the area where they are grown?
- How can I create clothes that can be safely composted when their materials cannot be cycled anymore?

"Thinking about system change allows me to prolong the emotional connection I have with my product by thinking about where it goes, who is going to own it, and how it is going to be used."

Patrick McDowell
Founder and Designer
Patrick McDowell

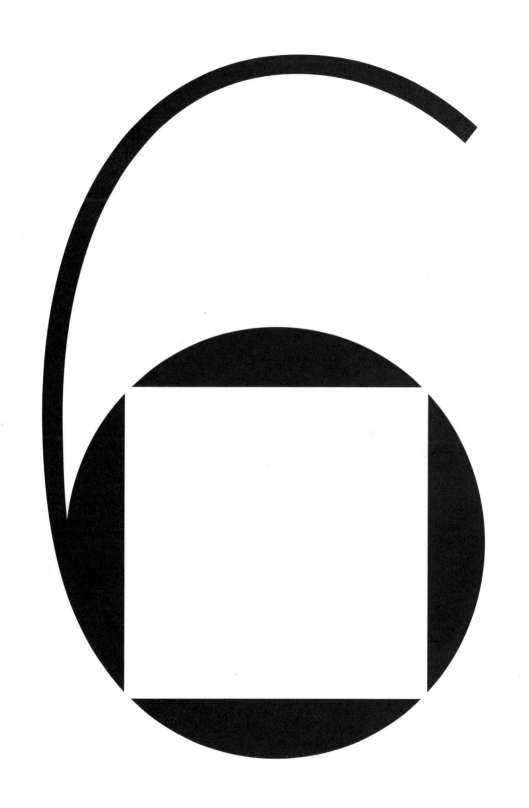

CONCLUSION

Advice from our contributors

"Think small and start at the core.

Taking action is the most important, otherwise you will start to overthink and get paralysed."

Duran Lantink
Designer

"People with ideas don't need advice.

Once they have found their lighthouse, they just need to follow their own light, unswayed by current trends."

Zhang Na
Founder
Reclothing Bank and Fake Natoo

"Designing for a circular fashion industry shouldn't be a competitive edge

— we can all be moving towards it together, educating each other

and sharing everything we know and what we've figured out along the way.

That's the vision: turning business into a force for good."

Eileen Fisher
Founder
Eileen Fisher

"Constantly think about how you can take your solution one step further

to ensure it will change the world for the better.

This may on occasion include throwing the rulebook out."

Eshita Kabra-Davies
Founder
By Rotation

"If you can achieve something for the greater good, that's what you should focus on."

Piyumi Perera
Head of Design Discovery Lab
Hirdaramani Group

"Do not stop exploring, researching and asking.

Do not hesitate to try something even if you think the market or your team is not ready.

Changes take time and require perseverance but will always arrive after some attempts."

Mariola Sánchez Morán
Sustainability Coordinator
Inditex — Oysho

"Learn from culturally diverse communities about their lifestyle and be intentional in what path you take to learn about circular design.

Embrace change and new innovative ideas that complement ancient ways of life that are true and tested."

Nimco Adam
Founder & Fashion Designer
QAALDESIGNS

"Ensure you bring everyone on board the circular journey from the start, clearly communicate to your wider team and supply chain what the end goal is, and collaborate with your broader network on how to get there."

Rebecca Garner
Circularity Partner
ASOS

"There is no such thing as perfection when it comes to circular design.

While we can strive for that, it is more important to start where you are and contribute where you can.

"It is the combination of all of us making small changes that finally makes a big impact."

Shobha Philips
Founder
Proclaim

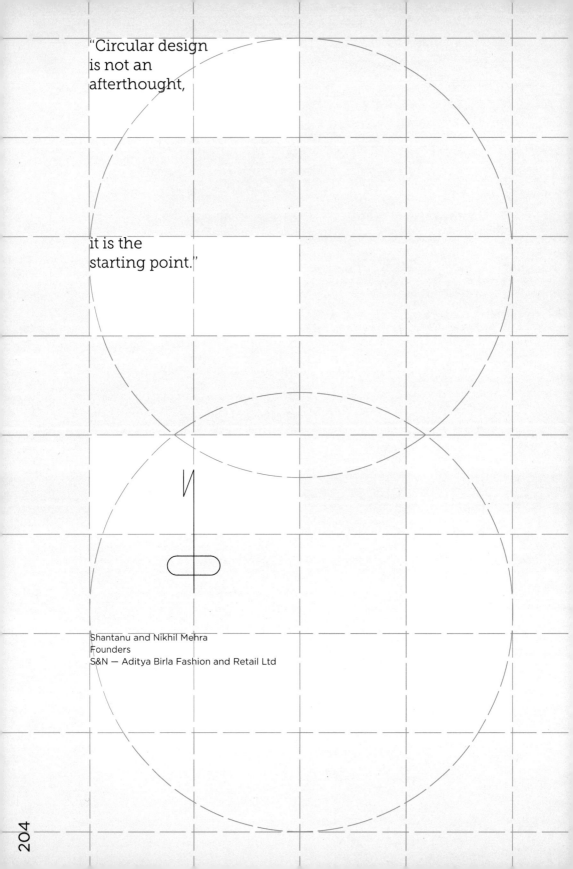

"Circular design is not an afterthought, it is the starting point."

Shantanu and Nikhil Mehra
Founders
S&N — Aditya Birla Fashion and Retail Ltd

Closing words   **Susannah Frankel**

Throughout my career I have seen how the fashion industry has, almost invariably, practised a linear model often without considering — or in many cases, even realising — the negative impact our behaviour might have on humanity, the catastrophic damage we are doing to our planet. The myriad voices brought together in these pages overturn the preconceived notions that have allowed this to happen. In so doing, they give us hope for the future — hope for a future that is aspirational and innovative for sure, but no longer at the expense of others; hope for a future that is uncompromisingly creative but without that going hand-in-hand with disastrous levels of waste and destruction.

The aim of this book is to fire the hearts and engage the minds of creatives throughout the fashion industry — to motivate us to work in an entirely different way. To move us, in every sense of the phrase.

Our future rests on the principles of a new practice, on a model that is as considered as it is considerate, as inspired as it is inspiring: on circular design practice. The brave and imaginative voices setting this agenda are gathered here: they are legion. By describing their journey towards transforming the fashion industry into a more responsible, thriving and caring place, they are paving the way for us all.

They have given us the tools, it is now for us to use them. In so doing, we hope, we can find equally creative and courageous methods of our own.

Glossary[51]

Composting

Composting is the process by which materials biodegrade through the action of naturally occurring microorganisms and do so to a large extent within a specified timeframe. The associated biological processes will yield CO_2, water, inorganic compounds, and biomass, which leave no visible contaminants or toxic residues.

Design for disassembly

Design principle that enables the product to be taken apart in such a way that components and materials can be reused, remade, or recycled.[52]

Durability

The ability of a physical product to remain functional and relevant over time when faced with the challenges of normal operation.

Microfibres

Textile fibres, or fragments of textile fibres, that are shed from the product during production, use, and after-use phases.

Recycling

The process of reducing a product back to its basic material level, reprocessing those materials, and using them in new products, components or materials.

Recycled material

Material that would have been disposed of as waste but is instead reprocessed by means of a manufacturing process and made into a final product or component for incorporation into a product.[53]

Regenerative production practices

Regenerative production practices build soil health and carbon content, increase water quality and biodiversity, and improve the resilience of ecosystems.

Remaking

Operation by which a product is created from existing products or components. This operation can include disassembling, re-dyeing, restyling, and other processes to improve emotional and physical durability.

Renewable material

Material that is composed of biomass from a living source and which can be continually replenished. When claims of renewability are made for virgin materials, those materials shall come from sources that are replenished at a rate equal to or greater than the rate of depletion.[54]

Repair

Operation by which a faulty or broken product or component is returned to a usable state.[55]

Reuse

Operation by which a product or component is used repeatedly and for long periods of time, for its original purpose, without being significantly modified, remade, or recycled. Products might need to be prepared for reuse, which often involves cleaning, repairs, or small modifications, so they can continue to be used over time and by multiple users.[56]

Traceability

The ability to trace products, components, and materials, as well as the social and environmental conditions in which they were made, along the whole supply chain, including after use.

Transparency

The ability to make information (for example on product specifications, chemical inputs, materials used, and production practices) available to all actors in the supply chain (including users), leading to common understanding, accessibility, comparability, and clarity.

Waste

Materials or substances that are discarded and no longer used, typically resulting in landfill, incineration, or leakage into the environment.

Acknowledgements

We are very grateful for the support we received in producing this book. To players of People's Postcode Lottery who made this book possible, to the Make Fashion Circular Advisory Board and participants for their ongoing support and active involvement, and to the many leading academic, industry, NGO, and government agency experts who provided invaluable perspectives.

We would also like to extend our gratitude to Amber Olson Testino and the Art Partner team for their unconditional support, to Susannah Frankel for the editorial direction, and to Ferdinando Verderi and Sara Sozzani Maino for their words. This book would not be the same without their extraordinary, artistic and insightful participation.

PHILANTHROPIC PARTNERS:

Laudes Foundation

MAVA Foundation

Players of People's Postcode Lottery

Expert contributors

adidas	Kristen Nuttall, Senior Designer Sustainability
	David Quass, Global Director Brand Sustainability
ADIFF	Loulwa Al Saad, Founding Team and Marketing Director
	Angela Luna, Founder and Creative Director
Aditya Birla Fashion and Retail Ltd	Ashish Dikshit, Managing Director
	Dr Naresh Tyagi, Chief Sustainability Officer
	Padmakar Pandey, General Manager, Sustainability
	Janet Arole, AVP & Head – Corporate Communications
Alvanon	Saúl Guzman, Communications Director
	Janice Wang, CEO
Art Partner	Amber Olson Testino, Founder
ASOS	Josie Ellis, Senior Garment Technologist
	Rebecca Garner, Circularity Partner
Atelier & Repairs	Maurizio Donadi, Co-founder
	Marisa Ma, Co-founder
Bank & Vogue	Steven Bethell, President and Partner
Bethany Williams	Bethany Williams, Founder and Designer
British Council	Hannah Robinson, Architecture, Design and Fashion Programme Manager
British Fashion Council	Caroline Rush CBE, CEO British Fashion Council
British School of Fashion, GCU London	Professor Natascha Radclyffe-Thomas, Professor of Marketing and Sustainable Business
Browns	Costanza Lombardi, Buyer Women's RTW
Burberry	Pam Batty, Vice President Corporate Responsibility
	Sinead Conway, Responsibility Programme Manager
	Vittoria Marchi, Responsibility Project Manager
	Jocelyn Wilkinson, Responsibility Programme Director
Bureau Betak	Alex de Betak, Founder and Creative Director
By Rotation	Eshita Kabra-Davies, Founder

Camera Nazionale della Moda Italiana	Paola Arosio, Head of New Brands and Sustainability Projects
	Carlo Capasa, Chairman
	Chiara Luisi, Sustainability Projects Coordinator
Candiani Denim	Danielle Arzaga, Blue Collars Srl Sustainability Manager
Central Saint Martins, University of The Arts London	Carole Collet, Director of Maison/0 and Co-Director Living Systems Lab, Central Saint Martins UAL
CFDA - Council of Fashion Designers of America	Steven Kolb, CEO Council of Fashion Designers of America
	Sara Kozlowski, Vice President of Education and Sustainability Initiatives
Circular Systems	Ricardo Garay, Agraloop Project Coordinator
	Linus Mueller, R&D Lead
	Isaac Nichelson, Co-Founder
Critical Textile Topologies	Dr Holly McQuillan, Zero Waste Design Researcher
DressX	Daria Shapovalova, Founder
	Natalia Modenova, Founder
Duran Lantink	Duran Lantink, Designer
Eileen Fisher	Eileen Fisher, Founder
	Carmen Gama, Design and Production Manager, Eileen Fisher Renew / Waste No More
EON	Natasha Franck, Founder and CEO
	Annie Gullingsrud, Chief Strategy Officer
Eugène Riconneaus	Eugène Riconneaus, Founder and Creative Director
FarFarm	Beto Bina, Founder
Fashion for Good	Georgia Parker, Innovation Manager
Fashion Revolution	Orsola de Castro, Founder and Global Creative Director
Fast Retailing	
Fédération de la Haute Couture et de la Mode	Pascal Morand, Executive President
	Léonore Garnier, Sustainability Project Manager
Ferdinando Verderi	Ferdinando Verderi, Creative Director
FFORA	Lucy Jones, Founder and CEO
Fibershed	Deborah Barker, South East England Regional Coordinator
	Emma Hague, South West England Regional Coordinator
Gabriela Hearst	Gabriela Hearst, Founder and Designer

Gap	Alice Hartley, Director, Product Sustainability, Gap Inc.
	Michele Sizemore, Senior Vice President, Global Product Development, Gap Inc.
	Kirsty Stevenson, Senior Director, Environment and Product Sustainability, Gap Inc.
Germanier	Kevin Germanier, Founder
Global Fashion Agenda	Jonas Eder-Hansen, Public Affairs Director
	Holly Syrett, Senior Sustainability Manager
Good American	Emma Grede, Founder and CEO
	Khloé Kardashian, Co-Founder
	Kristin Vander Ark, Denim Design Director
Gucci	Mich Ahern, Sustainability Communications Consultant
	Nevio Benvenuto, Head of CSR & Sustainability
H&M Group	Sarah Hayes, Business Expert for Circularity
	Petter Klusell, Design Function Manager, H&M
	Nellie Lindeborg, Sustainability Responsible Assortment, H&M
	Jasmine Qian, Research and Developer, H&M
	Ella Soccorsi, Senior Designer, H&M
	Cecilia Strömblad Brännsten, Environmental Sustainability Manager
	Anna-Karin Sundelius, Circular Strategy Lead
Hallotex	Sergi Masip Sanz, Circular Economy Project Manager
Hirdaramani Group	Thusitha Cooray, Chief Operating Officer
	Nikhil Hirdaramani, Director, Hirdaramani Discovery Lab
	Piyumi Perera, Head of Design, Hirdaramani Discovery Lab
ICICLE	Amos Zhang, Marketing Planning Manager
	Pupa Tang, PR and Communication Manager
	Zenobia Wang, Sustainability Officer
I:Collect GmBH	Paul Doertenbach, Managing Director
IDEO	Chris Grantham, Executive Director – Circular Economy
Institut Français de la Mode	Andrée-Anne Lemieux, Head of Sustainability IFM-KERING Research Chair
	Steven Kolb, CEO Council of Fashion Designers of America
	Xavier Romatet, Dean
Inditex – Oysho	Héctor Alonso Fernández, Sustainability Manager, Inditex
	Chisco García González, Manager of Sourcing and Sustainability, Oysho
	Iria Mouzo Leston, Head of Circularity and Global Sustainability Stakeholder Manager, Inditex
	Mariola Sánchez Morán, Sustainability Coordinator, Oysho
	Alfred Vernis Domènech, Senior Sustainability Manager, Inditex

Jaypore	Rashmi Shukla, Business Head, Jaypore, Aditya Birla Fashion and Retail Ltd
Kering	Sophie Bonnier, Head of Environmental Excellence and Circularity
	Marianne Franclet, Environmental Performance Manager
	Yoann Regent, Biodiversity and Animal Welfare Specialist
	Geraldine Vallejo, Sustainability Programme Director
	Nathalie Voisine, ESG and Corporate reporting
klee klee	Bu Wenxin, Merchandising Specialist
	Wang Yanyan, Brand Director
La Bouche Rouge	Nicolas Gerlier, Founder of La Bouche Rouge
Lacoste	Frederic Lecoq, Global Corporate Social Responsibility Vice President
	Catherine Spindler, EVP Marketing and Branding
Maggie Marilyn	George MacPherson, Communications
	Maggie Marilyn Hewitt, Founder and Designer
MARINE SERRE	Teresa Mereu, Head of Press
	Marine Serre, Founder and Creative Director
	Kelly Verny, Head of Legal and Corporate Social Responsibility Coordinator
Month Day Year	Noémie Balmat, Founder and CEO
Nkwo	Nkwo Onwuka, Founder
Orange Culture	Adebayo Oke-Lawal, CEO and Creative Director
Patrick McDowell	Patrick McDowell, Founder
Pepijn van Eeden	Pepijn van Eeden, Independent consultant, former CEO of MARINE SERRE
Phipps International	Spencer Phipps, Founder
Point Off View	Marina Testino, Creative Director, Artivist & Founder of Point Off View
	Paula Tovar, Agent Marina Testino
Powered by People	Ella Peinovich-Griffith, Founder and CEO
Proclaim	Shobha Philips, Founder
Provenance	Alanna Curtin, Client and Commercial Lead
	Sarah Fulton Vachon, Senior Marketing Lead
PVH / Tommy Hilfiger	Ariane Biemond, Senior Director, Tommy for Life
	Claire Boland, Director, Product Stewardship and Environmental Sustainability
	Laura Horvath, Manager, Sustainable Product
	Bill McRaith, former Chief Supply Chain Officer
	Esther Verburg, EVP Sustainable Business and Innovation
QAALDESIGNS	Nimco Adam, Founder and Fashion Designer

RÆBURN	Christopher Raeburn, Creative Director	
	David Segal, Digital and Creative Content Manager	
	Amelie Jannoe, Digital & Communications Coordinator	
Reclothing Bank and Fake Natoo	Zhang Na, Founder	
Redress	Hannah Lane, Strategic Director of Partnerships and Communications	
	Koey Wong, Education Manager	
Renewcell	Harald Cavalli-Björkman, Chief Marketing Officer	
RISE Worldwide — Lakmé Fashion Week	Jaspreet Chandok, Head of Lifestyle Businesses	
	Darshana Gajare, Head Sustainability	
	Kunal Wadhwani, Manager Sustainable Fashion	
RSA	Gabi de Rosa, Designer	
	Rebecca Ford, Head of Design and Innovation	
	Nat Ortiz, Senior Designer	
	Josie Warden, Head of Regenerative Design	
SAMUEL GUÌ YANG	Erik Litzén, Co-Creative Director	
	Caroline Wåglund, CEO	
	Samuel Yang, Founder	
Sara Maino		
Shanghai International College of Fashion and Innovation (SCF), Donghua University	Dr Jun Li, Dean, Associate Professor	
Shanghai Fashion Week	Xiaolei LYU, Deputy Secretary-General of Shanghai Fashion Week Organization	
Shantanu & Nikhil	Nikhil Mehra, Chief Design Officer	
	Shantanu Mehra, CEO	
Stella McCartney	Stella McCartney, Founder	
	Arabella Rufino, Worldwide Communications Director	
	Sarah Barnes, PR Manager	
Sellalong	John Atcheson, Co-Founder and CEO	
Style House Files — Lagos Fashion Week	Debola Adebowale, Project Coordinator	
	Omoyemi Akerele, Founder and Executive Director	
Susannah Frankel		
Taylor Stitch	Michael Maher, Co-Founder and CEO	
Teemill	Martin Drake-Knight, Co-Founder	
Textile Exchange	Liesl Truscott, Director of European & Materials Strategy	

The African Rack	Rudo Nondo, Head of Creative Design
The Fabricant	Kerry Murphy, Founder
The Renewal Workshop	Nicole Bassett, Co-Founder
The Restory	Thaís Cipolletta, Co-Founder and Head of Atelier
	Vanessa Jacobs, Founder and CEO
	Emily Rea, Co-founder and Head of Marketing and Business Development
The Sustainable Angle | Future Fabrics Expo	Nina Marenzi, Founder
thredUP	Samantha Blumenthal, Director, Marketing Communications
	Karen Clark, Vice President of Marketing Communications
	James Reinhart, Co-Founder and CEO
	Natalie Tomlin, Marketing Communications Manager
Tillmann Lauterbach	Tillmann Lauterbach, Creative Director
Timberland	Zachary Angelini, Environmental Stewardship Manager
Unmade	Ursula Davies, Vice President Sales
	Hal Watts, CEO and Co-Founder
Vestiaire Collective	Francesco Girone, Head of Communications and PR
	Sophie Hersan, Co-Founder
	Fanny Moizant, Co-Founder and President
	Dounia Wone, Chief Sustainability and Inclusion Officer
VF Corporation	Elisabetta Baronio, Sustainability and Corporate Social Responsibility Manager
	Marianella Cervi, Sustainability & Responsibility Senior Manager
	Massimo Ferrucci, President, Napapijri
Vivienne Westwood	Christopher Di Pietro, Global Brand Director
	Valeria Meliado, Senior Sustainability Fabric Researcher and Developer
	Vivienne Westwood, Founder
WGSN	Lorna Hall, Director Fashion Intelligence
W.L. Gore & Associates	Brian McAdams, Fabrics Durability Scientist
	Marie Måwe, Sustainability Stakeholder Engagement Director
YCloset	Stella Liu, Founder and CEO
Yehyehyeh	Shaway Yeh, Founder
YKK	João Matias, Sustainability Specialist

Ellen MacArthur Foundation Team

CORE PROJECT TEAM
- Elodie Rousselot, Circular Design for Fashion Programme Manager
- Egoitz Tellitu Diez, Circular Design for Fashion Analyst
- Cornélie Martin, Make Fashion Circular Analyst
- François Souchet, former Make Fashion Circular Lead
- Laura Balmond, Make Fashion Circular Lead
- Joe Iles, Circular Design Programme Lead
- Rob Opsomer, Executive Lead, Systemic Initiatives
- Andrew Morlet, Chief Executive

WITH SUPPORT FROM
- Marilyn Martinez, Make Fashion Circular Project Manager
- Chiara Catgiu, Make Fashion Circular Senior Analyst
- Matteo Magnani, Make Fashion Circular Senior Analyst
- Juliet Lennon, Make Fashion Circular Programme Manager
- Freya Amestoy, Make Fashion Circular Team Assistant
- Lauren Ward, Make Fashion Circular Team Assistant
- Claudia Fan, Senior Programme Officer
- Chuan Fan, Project Manager for Learning and Design
- Liansi Wang, Communications Manager, China program

EDITORIAL
- Ian Banks, Editorial Lead
- Tansy Robertson-Fall, Senior Editor
- Lenaïc Gravis, Senior Expert — Editorial
- Joanna de Vries, Editorial Consultant

MARKETING AND COMMUNICATIONS
- Nicola Evans, Marketing and Communications Lead
- Alix Bluhm, Communications Lead
- James Wrightson, Creative Lead
- Ross Findon, Media and Messaging Lead
- Rose Ely, Communications Manager
- Alex Hedley, former Creative Manager
- Sarah Churchill-Slough, Design and Branding Manager
- Emily Scadgell, Communications Executive
- Gabriella Hewitt, Media Relations Senior Executive

LEGAL	Holly Buckley, Senior Legal Counsel
	Jennifer Tyson, Legal & Contracts Advisor
	Eliza Killpack, Trainee Solicitor
	Hilary Osterman, Contracts Manager
DIGITAL PRODUCTION	Yunus Tunak, Digital Design Manager
	Victoria Deegan, Digital Programme Manager
	Dan Baldwin, Digital Designer
DESIGN BY SID LEE	Design Director: Marie-Elaine Benoit
	Graphic Design and Art Direction: Mélanie Boucher, Marie Chénier
	Illustrations: Marie Chénier, Benjamin Lamingo L'écuyer
	Coordination and Production: Marie-Christine Aucoin, Marie-Christine Côté, Annie Dufresne
PRINT PRODUCTION	M&H Polystudios
PRINTING	Seacourt
PAPER	Cover: 160gsm Elements Fire, 2250mic greyboard
	Interior: 120gsm FreeLife Cento Extra White
	Endpapers: 150gsm Recycled Pure Offset FSC Recycled. (100% Recycled Fibre Content)
TYPEFACES	Gotham, Museo Slab

Notes

1. Ellen MacArthur Foundation, *A new textiles economy: redesigning fashion's future* (2017), p. 18

2. Ellen MacArthur Foundation, *A new textiles economy: redesigning fashion's future* (2017), p. 36

3. Grandview Research, *Luxury apparel market share, industry report 2019-2025* (2019)

4. Ellen MacArthur Foundation, *A new textiles economy: redesigning fashion's future* (2017), p. 19

5. Barnardo's, *Once worn thrice shy* (2015); L.R. Morgan, and G. Birtwistle, *An investigation of young fashion consumers' disposal habits* (2009)

6. Textile Exchange, *Material change insights report 2019* (2020), p. 29

7. International Energy Agency, *Energy, climate change & environment: 2016 insights* (2016), p. 113

8. A.Granskog, et al. *Biodiversity: the next frontier in sustainable fashion*, McKinsey (23rd July 2020)

9. Ellen MacArthur Foundation, *A new textiles economy: redesigning fashion's future* (2017), p. 66; J. Boucher, and D. Friot, *Primary microplastics in the oceans: a global evaluation of sources.* Gland, Switzerland: IUCN (2017) pp. 21-22

10. R. Cernansky, It's time for fashion to remove toxic chemicals from clothing, Vogue Business (31st May 2019)

11. Ellen MacArthur Foundation, *A new textiles economy: redesigning fashion's future* (2017), p. 21

12. Fashion Revolution CIC, *Why we still need a fashion revolution* (2020), pp. 29-31

13. U.S. Department of Labor's Bureau of International Labor Affairs (ILAB), *2018 Findings on the worst forms of child labor* (2018); Anti-Slavery International and Embode Ltd, *Sitting on pins and needles: a rapid assessment of labour conditions in Vietnam's garment sector* (2018); Safia Minney, *Slave to fashion*, (accessed 30th November 2020)

14. See Greenpeace, *Eleven flagship hazardous chemicals*

15. KEMI, *Chemicals in textiles: risks to human health and the environment* (2014); Greenpeace, *Eleven flagship hazardous chemicals*; Changing Markets Foundation, *Dirty fashion: How pollution in the textiles supply chain is making viscose toxic* (2017)

16. van Eeden, P., *Upcycling end-of-life garments in contemporary fashion: the case of MARINE SERRE* (June 2021), Soulmachine, https://soulmachine.fr/articles.

17. Inclusive Design Toolkit, *Definition of inclusive design*, University of Cambridge (2017)

18. Inclusive Design Toolkit, *Understanding user diversity*, University of Cambridge (2017)

19. Wear Proclaim, *About* (2021)

20. L. Jackson, *Takafumi Tsuruta: not bound by the convention of disability* (25th March 2015)

21. M. McDowell, *Designers explore the future of digital clothing*, Vogue Business (4th April 2019)

22. R. Cernansky, *It's time for fashion to remove toxic chemicals from clothing*, Vogue Business (31st May 2019)

23. Ellen MacArthur Foundation, *A new textiles economy: redesigning fashion's future* (2017), p. 66; J. Boucher and D. Friot, *Primary microplastics in the oceans: a global evaluation of sources*, Gland, Switzerland: IUCN (2017). pp. 21-22

24. Inditex, *Annual Report 2019* (2019)

25. Kering, *Kering standards for raw materials and manufacturing processes* (July 2020)

26. Ellen MacArthur Foundation, *A new textiles economy: redesigning fashion's future* (2017), p. 37

27. ISPO.com, *Better fits: body data specialist Alvanon reconnects target groups and clothing collections* (26th January 2021)

28. Redress, *Zero-waste design technique* (2019)

29	L. Lewis, *Shima Seiki pins hope of fashion revolution on knitting machine*, Financial Times (27th June 2019)
30	Ellen MacArthur Foundation, *A new textiles economy: redesigning fashion's future* (2017), p. 77 (Circular Fibres Initiative analysis based on Euromonitor International Apparel & Footwear 2016 Edition (volume sales trends 2005-2015). (All numbers include all uses until the garment is discarded, including reuse after collection and resale.)
31	WRAP, SCAP textiles tracker survey, (2016)
32	WRAP, SCAP textiles tracker survey, (2016)
33	Ellen MacArthur Foundation, *A new textiles economy: redesigning fashion's future* (2017), p. 36
34	S. Halliday, H&M opens in hammersmith with new features to drive footfall, UK Fashion Network (10th December 2018)
35	H&M Group, H&M take care (12th December 2020)
36	Ellen MacArthur Foundation, *A new textiles economy: redesigning fashion's future* (2017), p. 37
37	L. Freeman, "Sustainable designs still have to be beautiful": MARINE SERRE on her upcycled SS20 Collection, Vogue (24th September 2019)
38	Ellen MacArthur Foundation, *A new textiles economy: redesigning fashion's future* (2017), p. 20 This includes recycling after use, as well as the recycling of factory offcuts. Expert interviews and some reports suggest that the rate of recycling clothing after use could be below 0.1% (see, e.g. A. Wicker, Fast fashion is creating an environmental crisis, Newsweek (1st September 2016)
39	EON, *CircularID* (2020)
40	Project Provenance Ltd, *About* (2021)
41	Project Provenance Ltd, *Increasing transparency in fashion with block chains* (2021)
42	N. Bruce, et al., *Microfiber pollution and the apparel industry* (2016), p. 3
43	Ellen MacArthur Foundation, *Cities and circular economy for food* (2019), p. 26
44	Rodale Institute, *Dig deeper: chemical cotton* (4th February 2014)
45	W. Bauck, *The next wave of sustainable fibre is all about regenerative farming*, Fashionista (27th March 2019)
46	Circular Systems, *Agraloop BioFibre™ The NEW natural fiber* (2020)
47	Mode In Textile, *Kering et le Savory Institute lancent le premier approvisionnement écologique certifié au sein de l'industrie de la mode* (7th December 2018)
48	Savory Institute, *Ecological Outcome Verification (EOV), version 2.0* (2019)
49	Donald H. Messersmith, *Lincoln Memorial lighting and midge study*, unpublished report prepared for the National Park Service, CX-2000-1-0014. N.p. (1993)
50	PhD Marketing, *The future of packaging design* (accessed 30th November 2020)
51	Ellen MacArthur Foundation, A vision for a circular economy for fashion (2020), https://www.ellenmacarthurfoundation.org/assets/downloads/Vision-of-a-circular-economy-for-fashion.pdf
52	ISO 14021:2016 (en) — Environmental labels and declarations — self-declared environmental claims (Type II environmental labelling), based on Section 7.4.1 Usage of term
53	ISO 14021:2016 (en) — Environmental labels and declarations — self-declared environmental claims (Type II environmental labelling), based on Section 7.8.1. Usage of terms
54	ISO 14021:2016 (en) — Environmental labels and declarations — self-declared environmental claims (Type II environmental labelling), based on Sections 7.14.1. Usage of term and 7.14.2. Qualifications.
55	BS 8001:2017 — Framework for implementing the principles of the circular economy in organizations — Guide, based on Section 2.56 Repair
56	Source: BS 8001:2017 — Framework for implementing the principles of the circular economy in organizations — Guide, based on Section 2.59 Reuse/reused

Photography

	SOURCE	CREDIT
004	Ferdinando Verderi	Ferdinando Verderi
006	Sara Sozzani Maino	Rosi di Stefano
014	Shutterstock	Carlos Baeza Ortega
018 — 019	Shutterstock	Varandah
020, 027	Shutterstock	Prapann
021, 196, 201	Shutterstock	Rob D the Baker
028 (below)	Shutterstock	Winnievinzence
028 — 029	Shutterstock	Sergey Bogomyako
032 — 033	Shutterstock	koTRA
056	Bethany Williams	Studio Rogue, Rory Gullan
060	Renewcell	Renewcell
064	Outland Denim	Elisabeth Willis Photography, Elisabeth Dodd
066 (1)	Mud Jeans	Recycle Factory Recover
066 (2)	Mud Jeans	Recycle Factory Recover
066 (3)	Mud Jeans	Recycle Factory Recover
066 (4)	Mud Jeans	Recycle Factory Recover
067 (5)	Mud Jeans	Recycle Factory Recover
067 (6)	Mud Jeans	Weaving Factory Tejidos Royo
068 (7)	Mud Jeans	Weaving Factory Tejidos Royo
068 (8)	Mud Jeans	Weaving Factory Tejidos Royo
069 (9)	Mud Jeans	Weaving Factory Tejidos Royo
070 (10)	Mud Jeans	Stitching and Washing Factory Yousstex International
070 (11)	Mud Jeans	Stitching and Washing Factory Yousstex International
071	Tommy Hilfiger	I Heart Studios
074 — 075	Atelier & Repairs	Trevor Pikhart
076	Adebayo Oke-Lawal	Michael Oshai
079	Duran Lantink	Paul Kooiker
090	Tillmann Lauterbach	Re;Re;Re; by Jnby
091 (above)	Patrick McDowell	Aaron Bird
091 (below)	Nimco Adam	QAALDESIGNS, Nimco Adam

094	Orange Culture	Michael Oshai
096 (above)	Bethany Williams	Melissa Kitty Jarram
096 (below)	Powered by People, Carolina Basilio	PaisTextil., Federico Romero
097 (above)	Orange Culture	Michael Oshai
097 (below)	Duran Lantink	Abel Minnee
098	Duran Lantink	Abel Minnee
099	Duran Lantink	Abel Minnee
100	Bethany Williams	Studio Rogue, Rory Gullan
101	Reclothing Bank, Zhang Na	Weirdo Cui
102	Klee Klee 2019 Spring/Summer Collection	Wang Yishu
104 (above)	Good American	Jamie Girdler
104 (below)	FFORA	The Sisters Elefterin, Zoe and Ari Elefterin
105 (above)	Proclaim	Proclaim
105 (below)	Getty Image	Yoshikazu Tsuno
106	Gabriela Hearst	Christina Fragkou
107	Germanier	Alexandre Haefeli
108	Ræburn	Ben Broomfield
114	Icicle	Courtesy of Icicle
116	Nkwo Onwuka	Mide King Visuals
118	Gabriela Hearst	Gabriela Hearst
128 (above)	Getty Image	Polly Borland
128 (below)	Alex de Betak	Bureau Betak
135	Shantanu&Nikhil	Shantanu&Nikhil, In-house team
136	Zhang Na	Li Kai
138	Samuel Gui Yang	Thue Nørgaard.
139	Samuel Gui Yang	Thue Nørgaard.
140	Germanier	Alexandre Haefeli
166	Rudo Nudo	Afrotography Images
163	Critical textile Topologies	Holly McQuillan
168	Stella McCartney	Dougal MacArthur
180	Bethany Williams	Natalie Hodgson
182	MARINE SERRE	MARINE SERRE
192	HNST Jeans	Studio Jef Claes
206	Susannah Frankel	Axel Drury

Bibliography

A

Anti-Slavery International and Embode Ltd, *Sitting on pins and needles — a rapid assessment of labour conditions in Vietnam's garment sector* (2018)

B

Barnardo's, *Once worn thrice shy*, Barnado's press release (2015) http://www.barnardos.org.uk/news/press_releases.htm?ref=105244

Bauck, W., *The next wave of sustainable fibre is all about regenerative farming*, Fashionista, (27th March 2019) https://fashionista.com/2019/03/regenerative-agriculture-farming-sustainable-fashion

Boucher, J., and Friot, D., *Primary microplastics in the oceans: a global evaluation of sources*, Gland, Switzerland: IUCN (2017)

Bruce, N., et al., *Microfiber pollution and the apparel industry* (2016)

C

Cernansky, R., *It's time for fashion to remove toxic chemicals from clothing*, Vogue Business (31st May 2019) https://www.voguebusiness.com/technology/fashion-remove-toxic-chemicals-from-clothing

Circular Systems, *Agraloop BioFibre™ the NEW natural fiber*, website (2020), https://circularsystems.com/agraloop

E

Ellen MacArthur Foundation, *A new textiles economy: redesigning fashion's future* (2017)

Ellen MacArthur Foundation, *A vision for a circular economy for fashion* (2020), https://www.ellenmacarthurfoundation.org/assets/downloads/Vision-of-a-circular-economy-for-fashion.pdf

Ellen MacArthur Foundation, *Cities and circular economy for food* (2019)

Ellen MacArthur Foundation and IDEO, https://www.circulardesignguide.com/

EON, *Circular ID* (2020), https://www.eongroup.co/circularid

Euromonitor, *International apparel & footwear, 2016 Edition* (volume sales trends 2005-2015) (2016)

F

Fashion Revolution CIC, *Why we still need a fashion revolution* (2020), https://www.fashionrevolution.org/why-do-we-need-a-fashion-revolution/

Freeman, L., *"Sustainable designs still have to be beautiful": MARINE SERRE on her upcycled SS20 Collection*, Vogue (24th September 2019) https://www.vogue.co.uk/fashion/article/marine-serre-on-her-upcycled-ss20-collection-paris-fashion-week

G

Grandview Research, *Luxury pparel Market Share, Industry Report 2019-2025* (2019), https://www.grandviewresearch.com/industry-analysis/luxury-apparel-market/toc

Granskog, A., et al. Biodiversity: *The next frontier in sustainable fashion*, McKinsey (23rd July 2020), https://www.mckinsey.com/industries/retail/our-insights/biodiversity-the-next-frontier-in-sustainable-fashion

H

H&M Group, *H&M Take Care* (accessed 12th December 2020), https://www2.hm.com/en_gb/free-form-campaigns/takecare.html/

H&M Group, *Sustainability performance report 2020* (2020), https://hmgroup.com/wp-content/uploads/2021/03/HM-Group-Sustainability-Performance-Report-2020.pdf

Halliday, S., *H&M opens in hammersmith with new features to drive footfall*, UK Fashion Network (10th December 2018), https://uk.fashionnetwork.com/news/H-m-opens-in-hammersmith-with-new-features-to-drive-footfall,1043745.html

I

Inclusive Design Toolkit, *Definition of inclusive design*, University of Cambridge (2017), http://www.inclusivedesigntoolkit.com/whatis/whatis.html#p30

Inclusive Design Toolkit, *Understanding user diversity*, University of Cambridge (2017), http://www.inclusivedesigntoolkit.com/whatis/whatis.html#p30

Inditex, *Annual report 2019* (2019)

International Energy Agency, *Energy, climate change & Environment: 2016 insights* (2016)

ISPO, *Better fits: body data specialist Alvanon reconnects target groups and clothing collections* (26th January 2021), https://www.ispo.com/en/promotion/alvanon/better-fits-body-data-specialist-alvanon-reconnects-target-groups-and-apparel

J

Jackson, L., *Takafumi Tsuruta: not bound by the convention of disability* (25th March 2015), http://www.thegirlwiththepurplecane.com/2015/03/25/takafumi-tsuruta-tenbo/

K

Kering, *Kering standards for raw materials and manufacturing processes* (July 2020)

L

Lewis, L., *Shima Seiki pins hope of fashion revolution on knitting machine*, Financial Times (27 June 2019), https://www.ft.com/content/8d03bfae-4a3a-11e9-bde6-79eaea5acb64

M

McDowell, M., *Designers explore the future of digital clothing*, Vogue Business (4th April 2019), https://www.voguebusiness.com/technology/digital-fashion-virtual-clothing-3d-design

Messersmith, Donald H., *Lincoln Memorial lighting and midge study*, unpublished report prepared for the National Park Service, CX-2000-1-0014. N.p (1993)

Minney, S., *Slave to fashion* (accessed 30th November 2020), https://safia-minney.com/slave-to-fashion/

Mode In Textile, *Kering et le Savory Institute lancent le premier approvisionnement écologique certifié au sein de l'industrie de la mode* (7th December 2018), https://www.modeintextile.fr/kering-savory-institute-lancent-premier-approvisionnement-ecologique-certifie-sein-de-lindustrie-de-mode/

P

PhD Marketing, *The future of packaging design* (accessed 30th November 2020), https://www.phdmarketing.co.uk/the-future-of-packaging-design/

Project Provenance Ltd, *About* (2021), https://www.provenance.org/about

Project Provenance Ltd, *Increasing transparency in fashion with block chains* (2021), https://www.provenance.org/case-studies/martine-jarlgaard

PwC Australia and Centre for Inclusive Design, *The benefit of designing for everyone* (2019)

R

Redress, *Zero-Waste design technique* (2019)

Rodale Institute, *dig deeper: chemical cotton* (4th February 2014), http://rodaleinstitute.org/chemical-cotton

S

Savory Institute, *Ecological outcome verification (EOV)*, Version 2.0 (June 2019), https://savory.global/wp-content/uploads/2019/12/EOV-manual-June-2019.pdf

T

Textile Exchange, *Material Change Insights Report 2019* (2020)

U

US Department of Labor's Bureau of International Labor Affairs (ILAB), *2018 findings on the worst forms of child labor* (2018)

V

van Eeden, P., *Upcycling end-of-life garments in contemporary fashion: the case of MARINE SERRE* (June 2021), Soulmachine, https://soulmachine.fr/articles.

W

Wear Proclaim, *About* (2021), https://www.wearproclaim.com/pages/about

Wicker, A., *Fast fashion is creating an environmental crisis*, Newsweek (1st September 2016), https://www.newsweek.com/2016/09/09/old-clothes-fashion-waste-crisis-494824.html

WRAP, *SCAP textiles tracker survey* (2016)

This book has been produced by the Ellen MacArthur Foundation (the Foundation). The Foundation has exercised care and diligence in the preparation of this book, and it has relied on information it believes to be reliable. However, the Foundation makes no representations and provides no warranties to any party in relation to any of the content of the book. The Foundation (and its related people and entities and their employees and representatives) shall not be liable to any party for any claims or losses of any kind arising in connection with or as a result of use of or reliance on information contained in this book, including but not limited to lost profits and punitive or consequential losses.

Visit the Circular Design for Fashion website to keep deepening your knowledge and learn from other practitioners in the industry.

https://circulardesignfashion.emf.org/